WORDS

PALMETTO
PUBLISHING
Charleston, SC
www.PalmettoPublishing.com

Words

Copyright © 2023 by Rick VanderHorst

All rights reserved
No portion of this book may be reproduced, stored in a retrieval system, or transmitted in any form by any means–electronic, mechanical, photocopy, recording, or other–except for brief quotations in printed reviews, without prior permission of the author.

First Edition

Hardcover ISBN: 979-8-8229-3199-2
Paperback ISBN: 9979-8-8229-3200-5

WORDS
Rick VanderHorst

Preface

I recently reflected on what was referred to as the Seven Wonders of the World which included the Great Wall of China, Petra and Machu Picchu to name a few. All are buildings, structures or monuments, feats of engineering from past civilizations.

As I contemplated mankind's greatest contributions, in general, I asked myself what was the greatest invention in terms of positively impacting human existence?

Was it the internet?

Could it be the combustible engine?

Was it something as simple as the wheel or could it be aerospace technology?

After giving it a lot of thought I came to the conclusion that the "written word" was the one innovation that differentiated us as a species.

That form of communication was unique and gave us the capability of cataloguing information, discoveries and analysis that could be passed on to future generations. It provides the adhesive for the advancement of societies and civilizations.

Words, specifically the written word, is the first Wonder of the World. This book is a celebration of words which, if chosen carefully, can heal, lift and open hearts.

Forward

In Jennifer, I had found the love of my life. It was chronicled in a series of 183 love letters written to her between 2018 and November 11, 2019, our wedding day. That day was the culmination of all my dreams.

Our love letters fill the pages of "Words". They came from the heart and serve as a reminder of how much I love her and how profoundly she has changed my life.

It is a love story that will live forever.

Contents

Chapter 1: Words 1

Chapter 2: I Found You 3

Chapter 3: Dreams 5

Chapter 4: Angels 7

Chapter 5: Wings 10

Chapter 6: To Rick 12

Chapter 7: Our Walk 14

Chapter 8: Listening 16

Chapter 9: Fearless 18

Chapter 10: " What If " 20

Chapter 11: Muse 23

Chapter 12: You Make Me Better 25

Chapter 13: You Have My Heart 27

Chapter 14: Zodiac 29

Chapter 15: Lost in You 31

Chapter 16: Poetry 33

Chapter 17: September 1971 35

Chapter 18: Tulips September 71'...........................37

Chapter 19: Gravity.. 38

Chapter 20: Your Eyes 40

Chapter 21: Only You 42

Chapter 22: I Choose You 44

Chapter 23: Music 46

Chapter 24: Soft Sighs 48

Chapter 25: Dance 50

Chapter 26: A Message from Heaven 52

Chapter 27: Unconditional Love 55

Chapter 28: Next To You..57

Chapter 29: Spirituality 59

Chapter 30: Your Journey 61

Chapter 31: The Key..63

Chapter 32: Twin Flames...................................... 66

Chapter 33: Finding You..69

Chapter 34: The Same Direction 71

Chapter 35: Forever 74

Chapter 36: Soulmate 76

Chapter 37: Sharing One Soul 78

Chapter 38: Finding You Was Fate........................ 80

Chapter 39: You Own My Heart..............................82

Chapter 40: My Love Story 84

Chapter 41: Infinity 86

Chapter 42: Laughter 87

Chapter 43: Best Friends..89
Chapter 44: Miracles.. 91
Chapter 45: Marry Me..93
Chapter 46: "Us" 95
Chapter 47: Sleepovers 97
Chapter 48: Sunsets... 99
Chapter 49: Old Friends 101
Chapter 50: Eternity 103
Chapter 51: Perfect 105
Chapter 52: Your Spirit 107
Chapter 53: The Miracle is You 109
Chapter 54: Lifetimes..111
Chapter 55: My Reset 113
Chapter 56: Only Goodnight...115
Chapter 57: Connection 117
Chapter 58: Shout! 119
Chapter 59: Life Together 121
Chapter 60: True Love Stories.. 123
Chapter 61: What's Next.. 125

CHAPTER 1

Words

The origins of the written language have been traced to around 3400 BC, in Persia.

Its significance is so important that prehistory is defined as human existence from the time we started using stone tools until we began to write.

Words represent the beginning of the history of mankind.

Writing is the encoding of the spoken language. It allows you to reconstruct thoughts, to relay impressions and even speak from the grave.

It gives an individual a vehicle to communicate knowledge, transmit information and speak from the heart.

Words can be the greatest gift that one can bestow on those they love.

If written down, they can be as lasting as a diamond.

Some say that, "A word is dead when it is said". I believe that it just begins the day you write it down.

Words can be a window into your soul. They remind us of what is in our hearts.

When written down, they can last forever, so choose them wisely.

They can paint pictures and can touch those you love in unforgettable ways. They can allow you to live a thousand lives instead of just one. They rekindle memories and keep love from fading with time.

Words are instrumental in the expression of our thoughts and feelings. Words can light fires and fuel passion between lovers.

Words from the heart are thoughts that breathe and lift our awareness. I choose to write them down to help and inspire, to heal the wounds inflicted by life. Words are emotions, feelings, verbal hugs and kisses with a dash of dictionary.

The spoken word is heard.

The written word is felt. I want to plant my feelings in your heart and let you read them over and over again.

This is to make sure that you know that I will never forget you. Words of love continue on like the stars in the heavens.

CHAPTER 2

I Found You

Jen,
I found you because the entire world aligned
and conspired to help me find you.

I don't regret

a single moment

spent believing you

were right for me

I knew that we would
someday end up together
because what is yours
will find you......

Rick

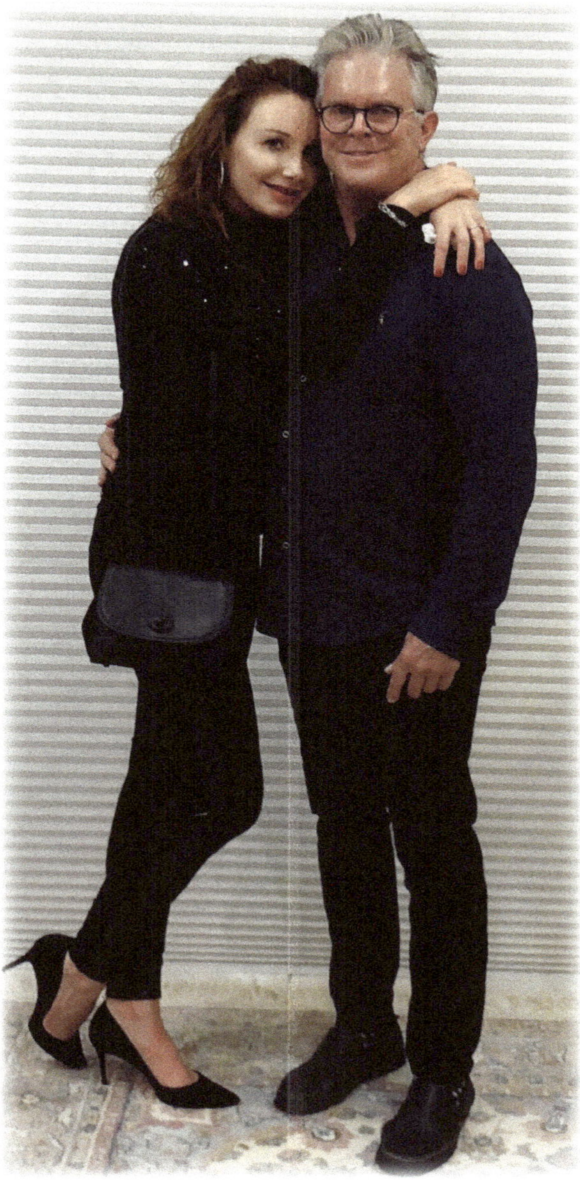

CHAPTER 3

Dreams

Jennifer,

Dreams are where we meet

when we are apart

Quiet your mind

Rest your heart.

No amount of guilt

can change the past.

No amount of anxiety

can alter the future

Yours is to live in the present

on the soft clouds of gratitude.

I love you

Rick

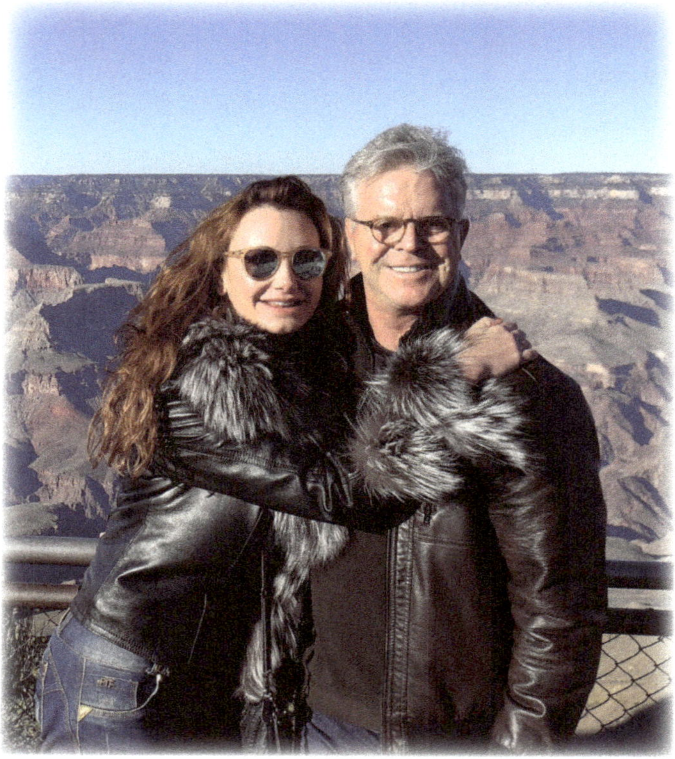

CHAPTER 4

Angels

I dreamt one night that angels came
to visit me in my sleep.

They told me about heaven.
I told them about Jennifer.

Angels are everywhere.
Many times
they are disguised as ordinary people.
Know that they are always watching
over you.

If you fall, they will pick you up.
If you can't go any farther,
they will carry you.
If you are tired,
rest in their arms.

I'm your guardian angel .
Whenever you see a white feather,
I'm telling you I'm close by.

If you cry during a sad movie,
I'm sitting next to you.
When you are inspired by
a beautiful song,
I'm whispering in your ear.

When you see a yellow rose,
My Mom is spreading her wings.

If you feel a breeze in your face,
I'm blowing you kisses.

If you see a hummingbird ,
my Dad is protecting you.

I will always love you.
I will always be there for you.

While you are sleeping
know that I am touching your soul
and holding you in my arms.

Rest

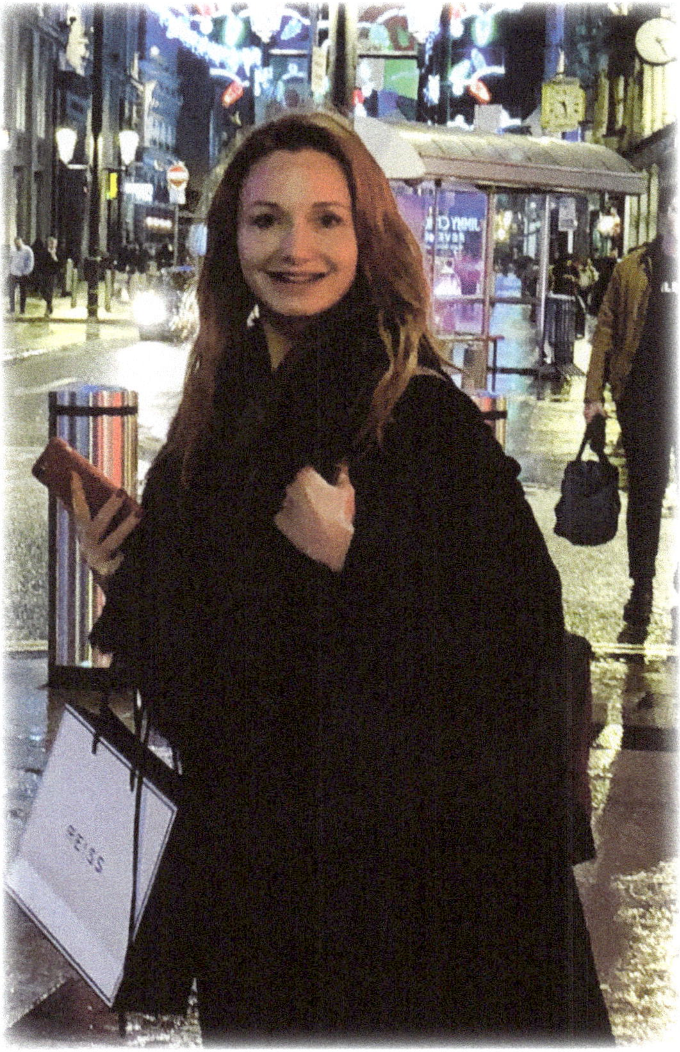
REISS

CHAPTER 5

Wings

Jen,

The angels brought us together so
you could heal my heart.
In turn, I am here to protect you,
to keep you safe.
They aren't going to let anything
happen to us.

I love you and I'm ready to start
a new life with you.
A life fuller than anything you or
I could have ever dreamt about.

What happens to others won't
happen to us.
We love each other in a more
passionate way.

I have no holes to fill.
I only want you.

Rick

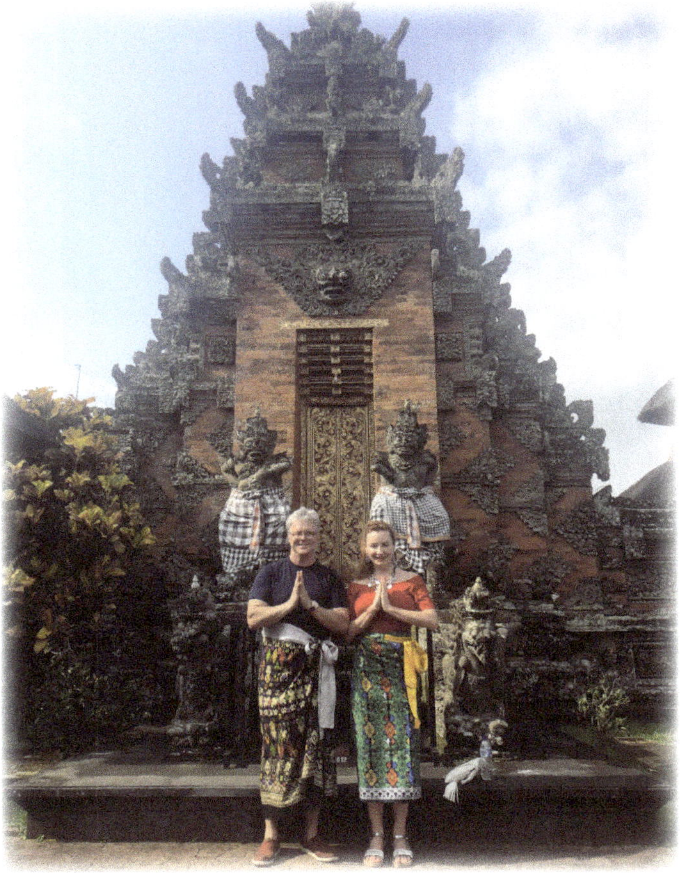

CHAPTER 6

To Rick

I know Babe. I love you so much and
I am teary eyed now.
I am looking
forward to spending my life with you!
You make me so happy.
I want only you too.
I didn't think about meeting the one
until you came along.
But meeting you has changed everything
for me.
I have never felt like this before.
You are the first and only person I
have ever felt I can go all the way with.
Rick, you are my soulmate.

Jen

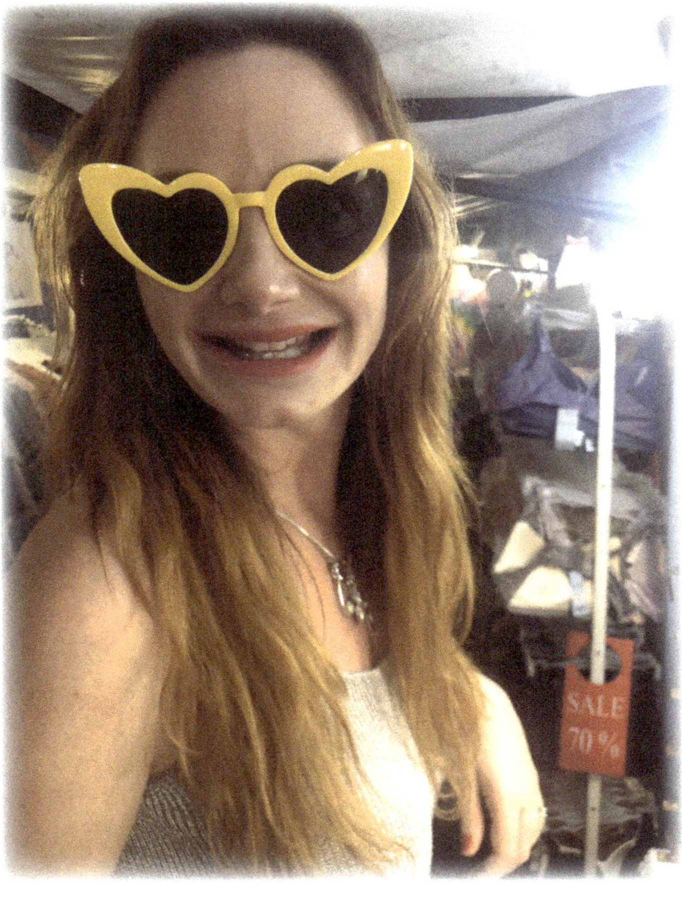
SALE
70 %

CHAPTER 7

Our Walk

Jen,

Being without you reminds me of
just how much you have added
to my life.

It is like walking into a room with
all the lights off.
Everything is the same
but there is only darkness.

I feel the joy that you add
and how much I miss it.

I just need you to know that
I love you more than words
could describe.

I don't mind losing sleep
over you.
You are my life.

Rick

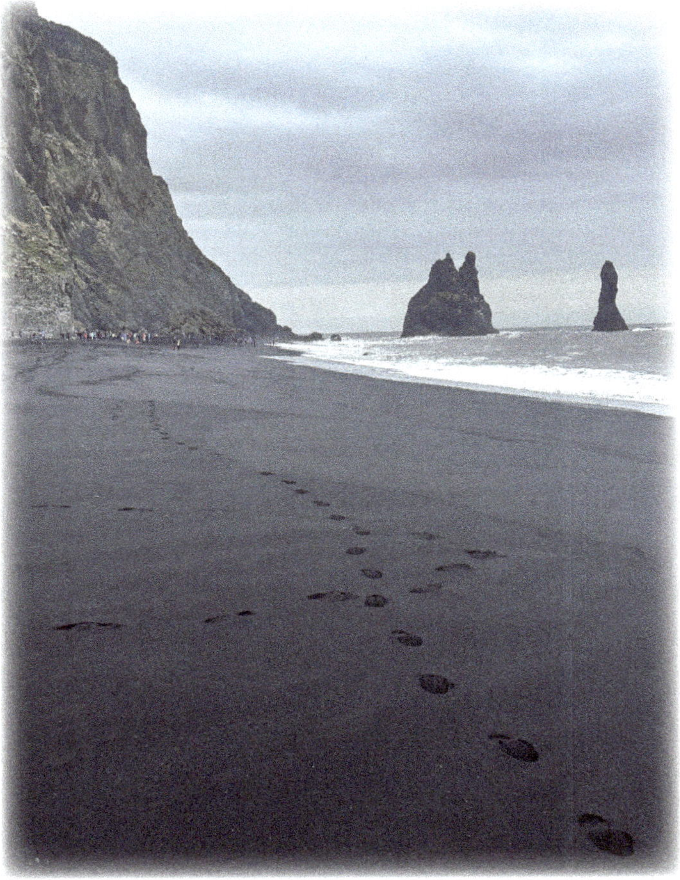

CHAPTER 8

Listening

Listening is an art. It is the foundation for communication. It is the most sincere form of respect to actually focus and concentrate on what someone else is saying to you.

Listening attracts and heals. It is the basis for learning. It is often what people need, others over self.

If you want to be listened to, You must first master the art of listening. Don't think or judge, just listen.

You will find that you will also hear things that, "aren't being said".

Most people don't listen with
the intent to understand. They
listen with the intent to reply.

I can promise you that Jen is
a great listener.
Never judgemental.
Only there to help.
She pays attention.
She cares.
She loves.

CHAPTER 9

Fearless

Jen,

You have found yourself. Knowing who
you are creates an inner strength.
It makes you fearless.
You lift everyone you touch.

My soul found you.
It recognised you immediately.
It had reunited with an old friend.
Someone that it had known over
many lifetimes.

Your growth has been trans-
formational.

When two souls reunite,
this is what happens.
You are simply amazing.
You are perfection.

Rick

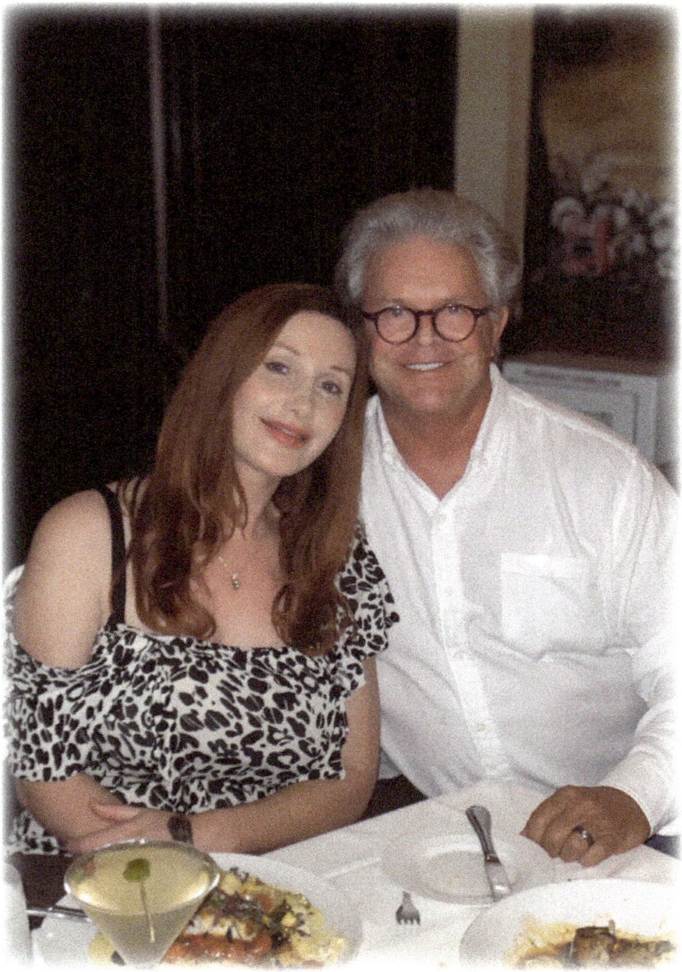

CHAPTER 10

"What If"

Jen,

Last night you asked me what I would do
if it didn't work out between you and I.
I didn't have a good response then but
When I woke up this morning the answer
was clear.

I would, first of all, find you in my dreams.
You had been there for years.
I loved you
then and I would simply reignite that love
affair all over again.

You helped me cope.
You were the voice
in my mind that helped to guide me through
difficult times.

Your face, your energy, the expectation of
finding you motivated me each and every
day.

I knew that you were out there and until
I found you, I lived my life largely in my
thoughts and I would go back there to you.

But then I would actually go do the things
that we talked about.
I would climb mountains
to see the sunrise.
I would walk on the beach
In Thailand and vacation in Bali.

I would go and see the world again and
imagine what it would be like to have you
next to me.
 I would spend the rest of my
life looking for your beauty in everything
around me.

Simply because every time I saw a
sunrise, every time I looked out over a
flower covered meadow, each time I saw
the emerald green waters coming on shore,
each time I saw something beautiful, it
would remind me of you.

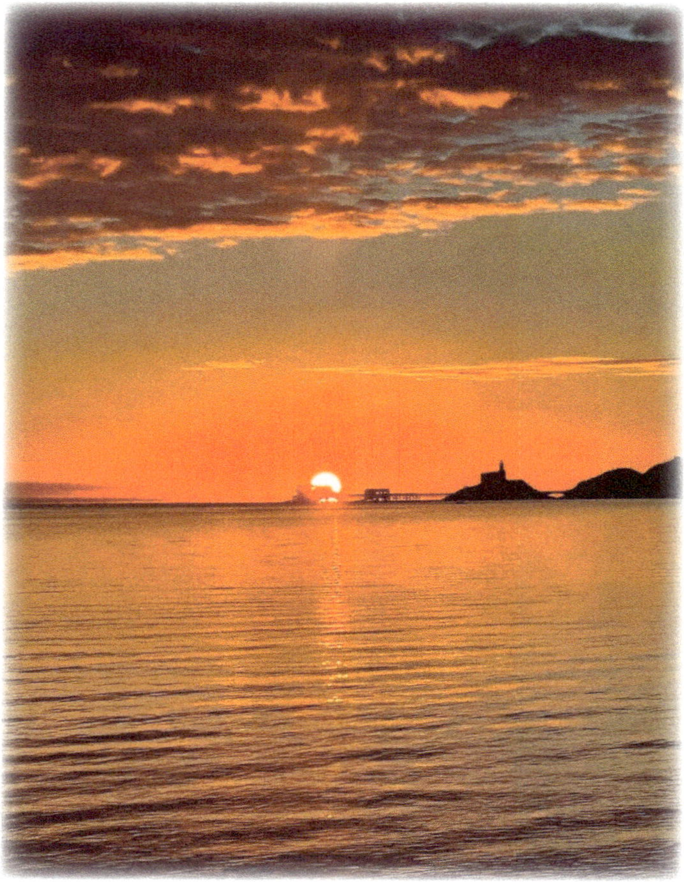

CHAPTER 11

Muse

Jen is the muse who sits on my shoulder. When I am immersed in my writing, she brings in the magic where angels fill in the blank spaces in my thoughts.

Her breath feels like an ocean breeze that relaxes and cools me.

She takes me to places I have never before seen and emotions I had never before felt.

Her gift is experienced in my words. Her guidance is my mirror.

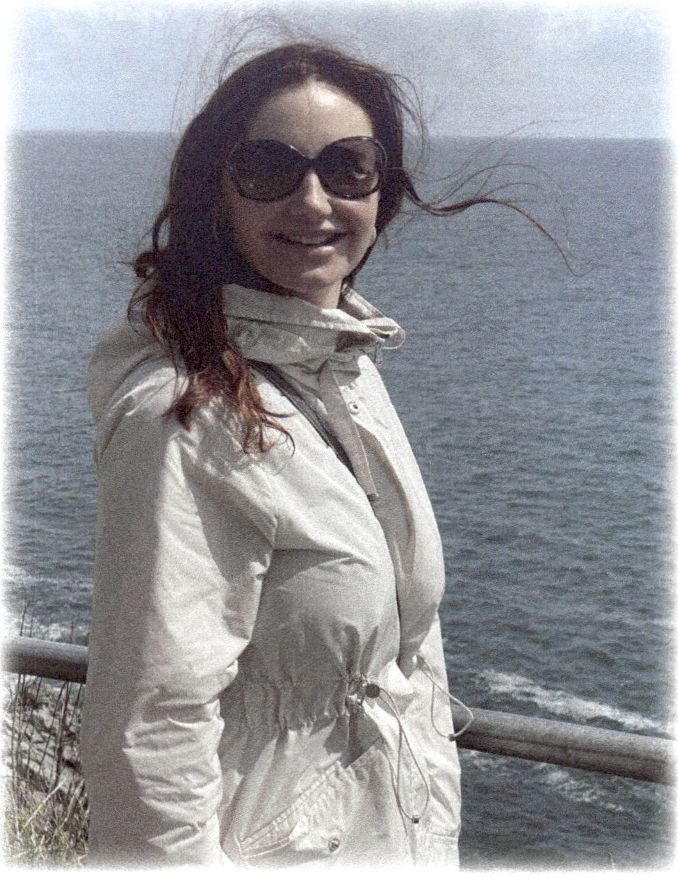

CHAPTER 12

You Make Me Better

Jen,

You make me better. You lift my thoughts. You heighten my awareness.

You raise me up to see the stars while keeping my feet planted solidly on the ground.

You've inspired me to look inside myself to find love and then share it with you.

Looking at things through your eyes has allowed me to find a new voice, to take on new challenges and to re experience life all over again.

Rick

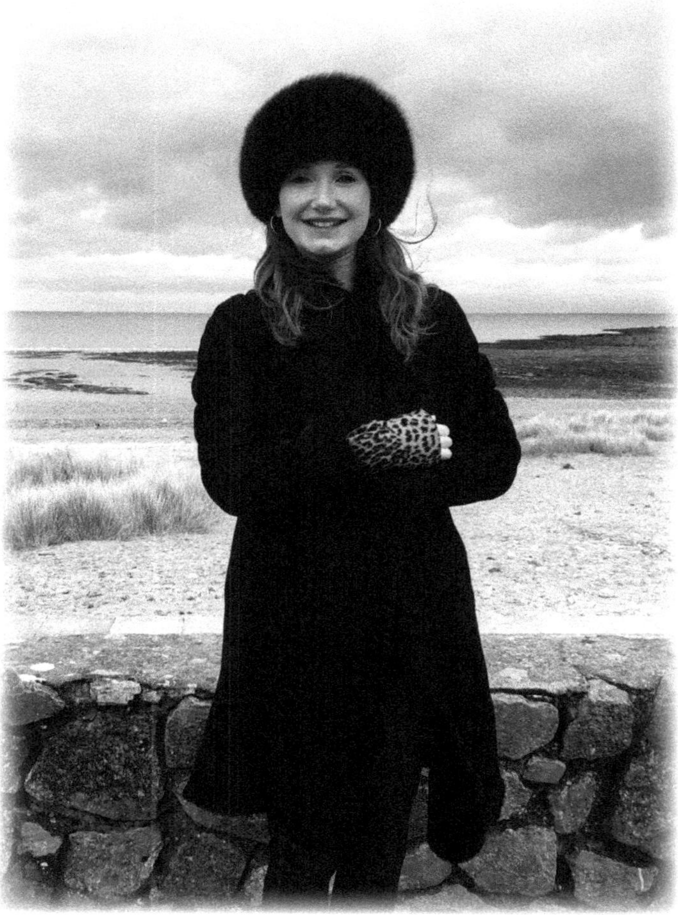

CHAPTER 13

You Have My Heart

Jen,

I fall in love with you again every single day.
I will be honest with you and true to the feelings that I had in making our love a reality.

If I ever did anything right in my life, it was when I gave my heart to you.

Only you can break it.
Only you can heal it.
That is why I can't ever see myself saying goodbye.

Rick

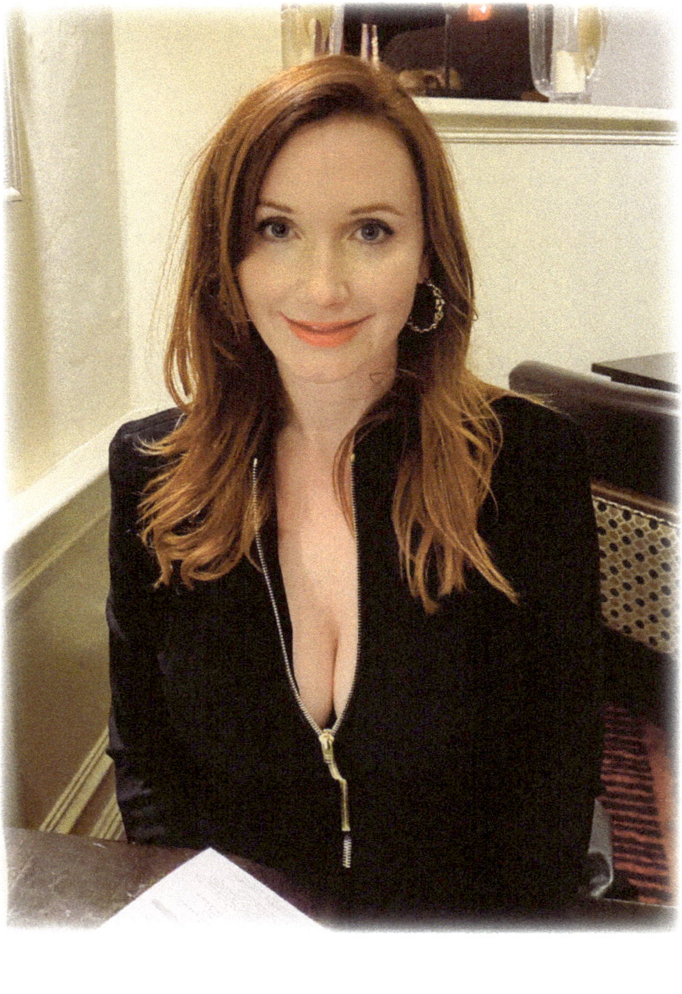

CHAPTER 14

Zodiac

"Gemini and Aquarius are a great match in love or friendship.
They make each other think, share intellectual interests, and admire each others independence.

These two understand each other on a deep level, and therefore have the potential for a magical relationship.

Gemini and Aquarius are almost perfectly compatible. These signs are constantly surprising one another. Both have a purpose in life to experience as many positive emotions and vivid impressions as possible."

As two Sun signs, they love and live to connect.

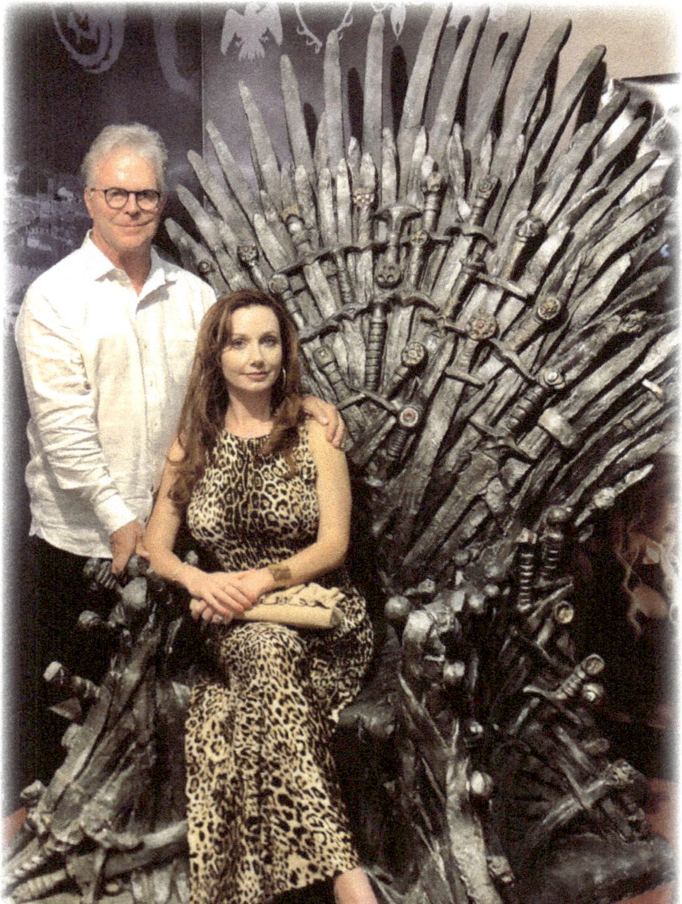

CHAPTER 15

Lost in You

Jen,

In getting lost in you,
I found myself again.

You are my love story.
I write you into everything I do,
everything I touch,
and all of my dreams.

You are the words that fill
the chapters of our story.
Our story is about intimacy.
It's about how you have changed
my life.

Love
Rick

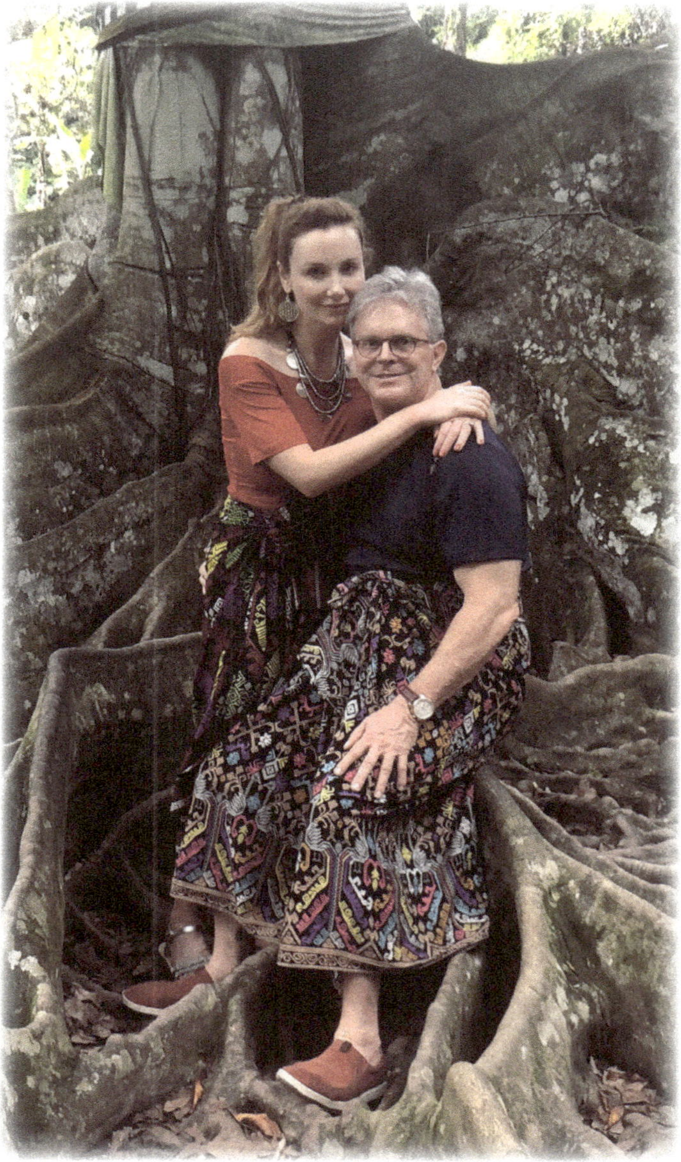

CHAPTER 16

Poetry

My first attempt at poetry was
a mere exercise in rhyme.

Painting strokes with a pen
in an effort to leave something
indelible on the heart.

Until I met you
I didn't know that poetry
was a living, breathing person.

After you
all words fall short.

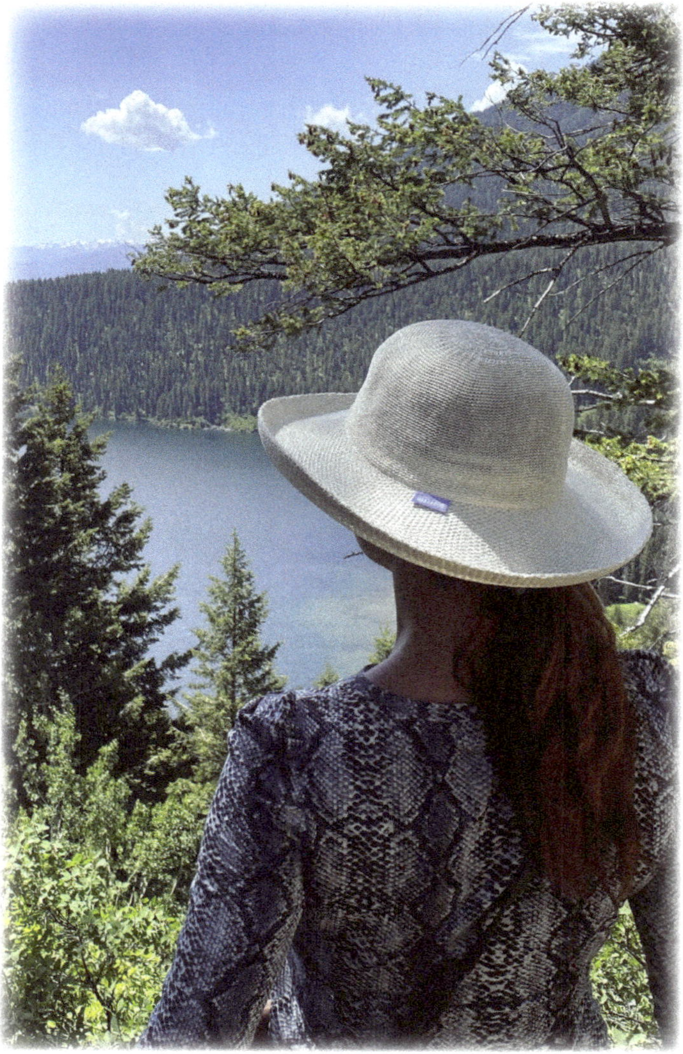

CHAPTER 17

September 1971

As the sands of the beach
meets the deep blue sea.
So natural it was
that you met me.

The love in my heart
grows like an on rushing wave.
Growing faster and faster
to the end I crave.

To flow across you
in a soft tender motion.
And pull you back with me
in loving emotion.

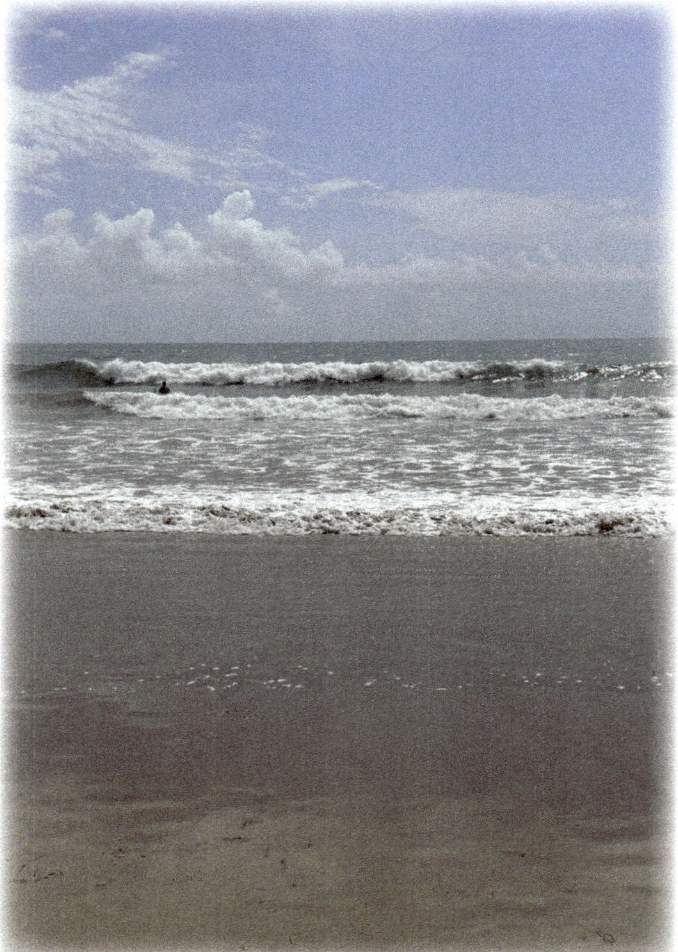

CHAPTER 18

Tulips September 71'

Tulips in the cemetery.
Tulips in the park.

But nothing is more romantic
then two lips in the dark.

CHAPTER 19

Gravity

The gravity of the past pulls us down.
Reflecting too much about what has
already happened keeps us from
moving forward in our lives.

Yesterday is for memories.
The future is for dreams.
The present is for you and me.

What has already happened gives
us a place to learn lessons.
But the gravity of the past should
not make us prisoners,
afraid to follow a new path together.

As you travel on our new journey,
pack light.
Let go of the things that no
longer serve you.

When we are caught up in the past,
We miss what's in our future.

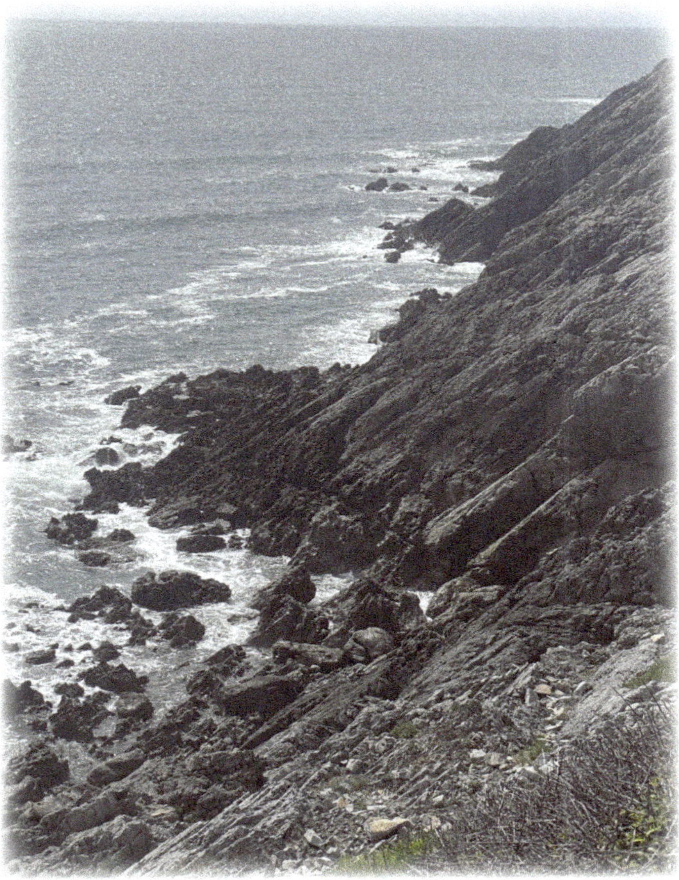

CHAPTER 20

Your Eyes

I look into your eyes
and see everything I need.
Your happiness has become
my happiness.

Your sadness is my pain.
You make me smile
even when you are not around.

You are the "happy pill"
that I take every day.
From the chaos of your mind
flows a soul of beauty and serenity.

You are a dichotomy
of strength and vulnerability.

Jen, you make me feel emotion,
see more vividly,
and experience a deeper sense of love
through our connection.

I carry you with me in my heart.
The day our eyes met,
my life began.

CHAPTER 21

Only You

Jen,

My heart beats only for you.
My eyes see only you.
My touch feels only your body .
My soul is yours.
I close my eyes at night
and only see you in my dreams.

I worship you in a way
that people are struck by a beautiful
sunrise or a valley full of flowers.

With you I can fly.
Because of you
I can touch the sky.

Rick

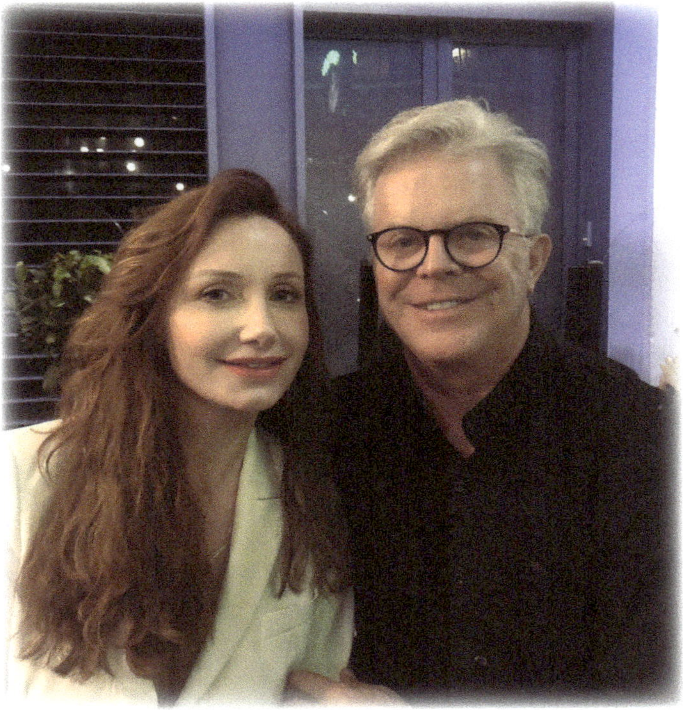

CHAPTER 22

I Choose You

Jen,

I choose you.
I only want you by my side.
In a dozen lifetimes,
in thousands of words,
no matter what was happening,
I would still choose you.

Our kind of love isn't something
you stumble across.
It wasn't an accident that we found
each other.

It was meant to be a continuation
of a life shared by twin flames
who refused to be apart.

You are the air that I breathe.
You are the best of my heart.
You are the twilight that over takes
me as I fall asleep.

You are the dream that makes me
want to never wake up.

I am yours
Rick

CHAPTER 23

Music

Music can tell a story that words simply can't.
Although songs are written for the public, some seem to be composed for just you and I.

We are connected through the songs that remind you of our times of joy, laughter and tenderness together.

It is a divine way to tell beautiful poetic things to the heart. I cannot think of anything that connects humanity more eloquently than a shared love of music.

We fell in love listening to Ed Sheeran. The words of his music spoke to our hearts and lifted our souls.

We look for the songs that touch us.
Songs that mend our hearts
and bring back memories.

When you are listening to the music
and tears come to your eyes,
know that I am whispering to your ear,
"I love you".

CHAPTER 24

Soft Sighs

Jen,

You have the ability to take me places
I have never been before.
You crawl into my mind
and make everything seem possible.

Your body speaks its own language.
Your touch ignites a depth of feeling
inside of me that jolts all my senses
and makes me more alive.

The soft sighs you emit when you
read our chapters,
your musical tones say that I have
touched your soul.

The emotion you feel from my words,
words carried on the wings of angels,
tells us that this was a connection
made in heaven.

We were meant to be together.
Rick

CHAPTER 25

Dance

Martha Graham said, "Dance is the hidden language of the soul".

Jen, who loves to dance, uses it to connect with her inner self, to open her up.

She would tell you that if you hit a wall, you can go over it, crawl under it or go around it.
She would want to dance on top of it.

If you are down, put on your favorite song. Close your eyes and dance like no one else is watching.

Become one with the music.
Cleanse your soul.
Find yourself by losing
yourself in dance.

If you need a partner,
know that I am there.

If God didn't give you wings to fly,
use your feet to dance.
It feels the same.

CHAPTER 26

A Message from Heaven

Jen,

Know that angels are carrying a message
of love to you from heaven.
They are taking my thoughts, my energy,
my love and putting them in words
that manifest in our story.

You dance inside my chest.
Your voice is my music.
You are not one in a million,
you are one in a lifetime.

When we began this journey,
I began to write our story knowing
that the last chapter had already
been written.

Our connection, our journey of
many lives together dictated the
inevitable.

We are going to enjoy each other
and take every moment to celebrate
our love until the day we stand on
the beach, you in your beautiful
white dress and declare our love
to the world.

The angels who have blessed us
with the inspiration are invited
to join us.

Rick

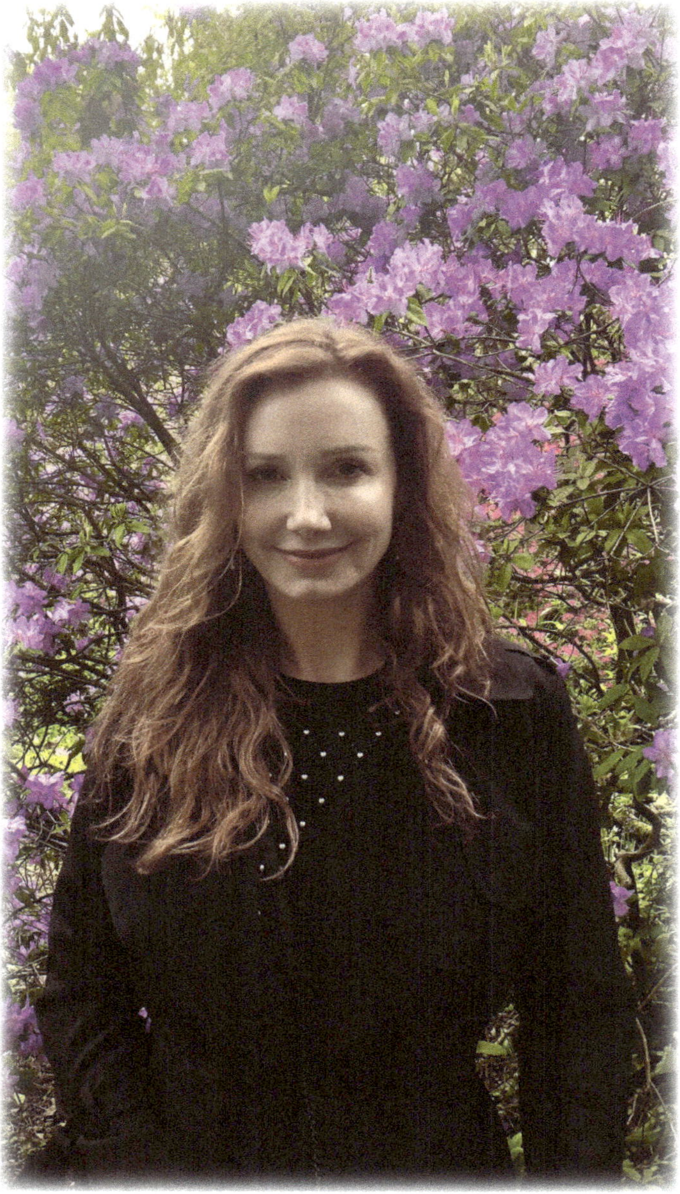

CHAPTER 27

Unconditional Love

"My love for you is unconditional."

You cannot do enough wrong to lose it.
You cannot make enough mistakes to
push me away. You cannot hurt me
enough to make me walk away.

You will make mistakes.
We will both make mistakes.
We will both create hurt
in some way,
at some point
in this life.

But, Jen, I will still love you.
Even if you hit a rebellious streak
and walk away or cut me out.

I will still love you.
I will always love you.
I could never stop loving you.

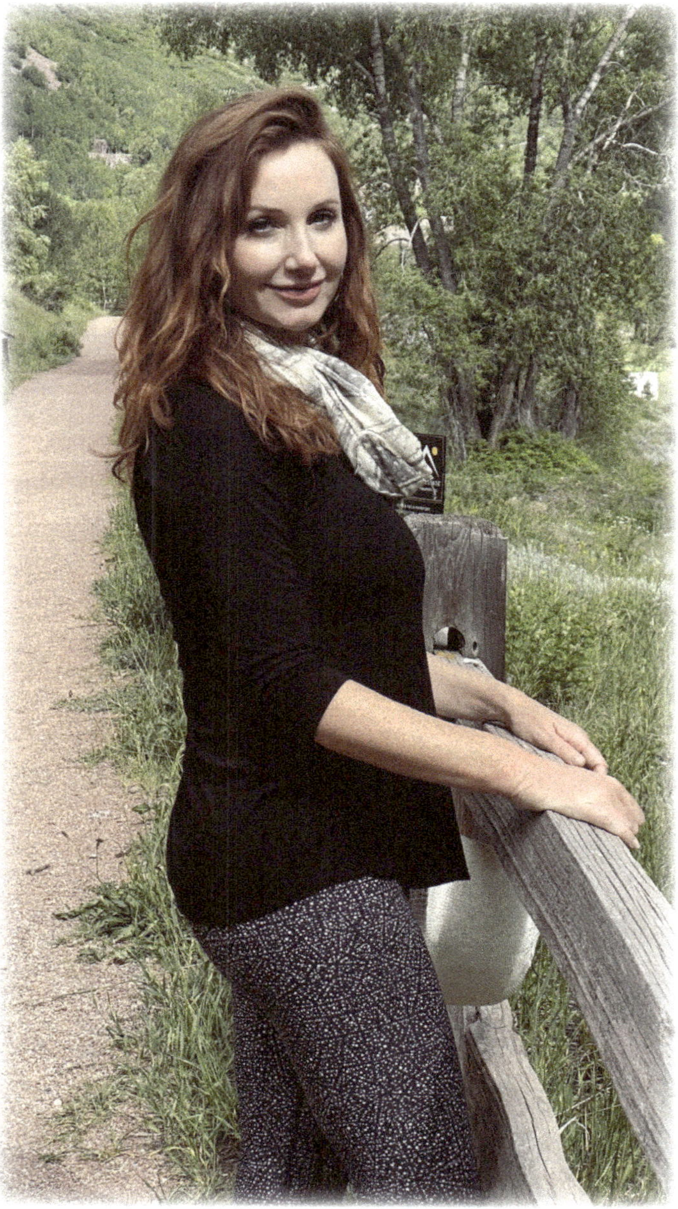

CHAPTER 28

Next To You

Jennifer,

I am standing in my favorite place in the world,
next to you.

I am lost in you
and I don't want to be found.

You have helped me realize that you never stop loving someone.
You either never did or you always will.

Of everything I've done in my life,
loving you was my greatest accomplishment.

Your happiness is my love story.

In order to have pure and unconditional
love that so few experience,
I need you right next to me.
I'm here

Rick

CHAPTER 29

Spirituality

"There is no other spiritual teacher than your own soul". Swami Virkamanda.

We carry within ourselves the answers. And it is from within that we can unlock the self love that is necessary to connect with the world.

So many work on their outward appearance in an effort to project attractiveness. Jen, you look inward to release the real grace and beauty in your soul.

Be grateful for all the obstacles in your life. They have strengthened you as you continue with your journey.

When we recognize that we are truly God's greatest gift, we can come to grips with the truth that no dream is too big and no level of happiness is unattainable in our lives.

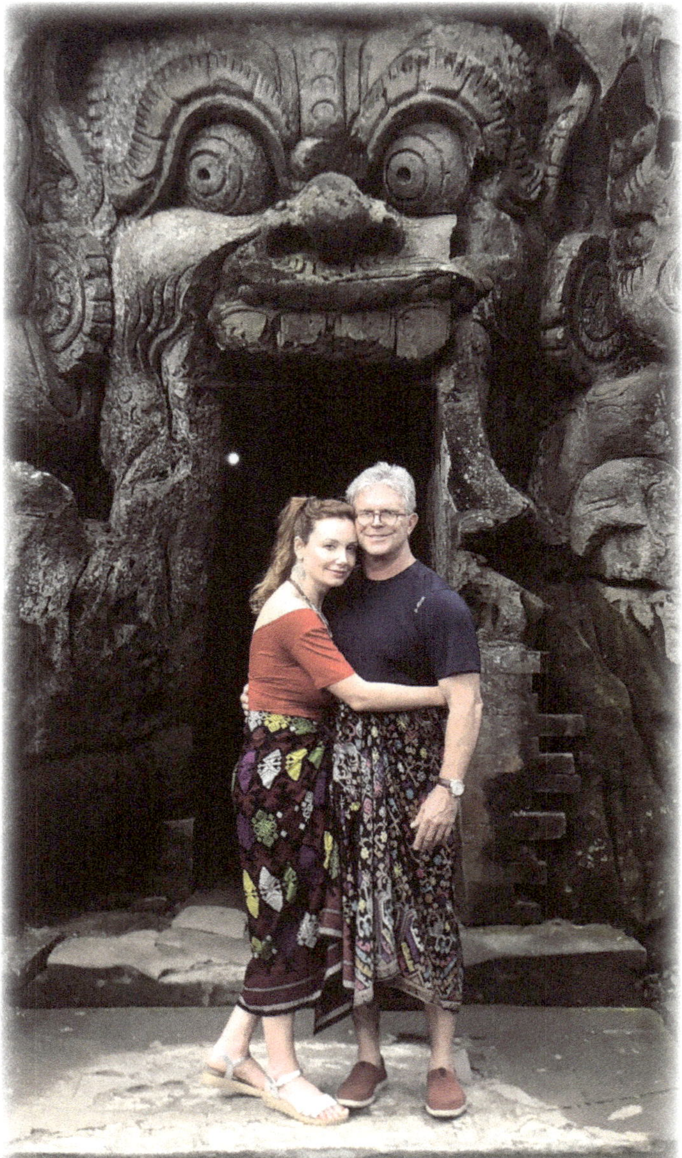

CHAPTER 30

Your Journey

Jennifer,

I understand your spiritual journey. I have faith in it. Everything had to happen exactly the way that it did in order for me to find you.

My journey was one of wandering. And everywhere I went you were on my mind.

The journey you are on seems to require that you walk alone. I sometimes sense the disconnect when you are on that path. But me letting go does not mean loving you less.

You becoming more yourself gives me more to love. I know that you are not afraid of repeating the past. I want you to grow. I want you to experience life. You deserve to be loved unconditionally. Enjoy your journey but always come home to me.

Rick

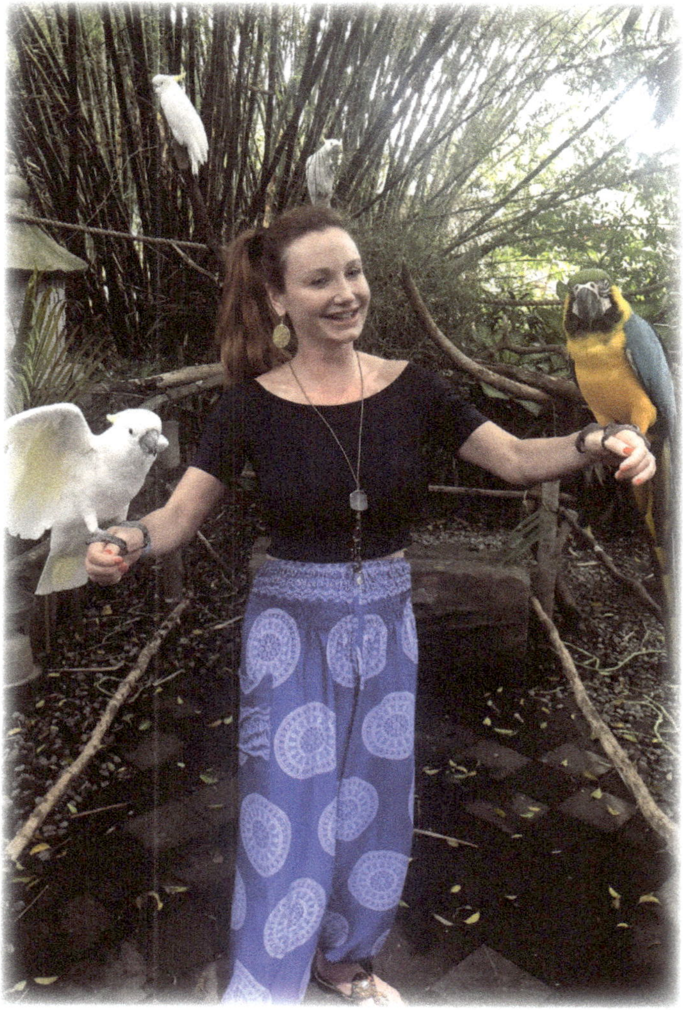

CHAPTER 31

The Key

Jenny,

It is difficult watching you struggle with unresolved issues from the past. There is a part of me that wants to protect you and keep you safe.

I don't have the answers and love has the capability to cloud one's judgement the same as anything else that influences our vision.

The answer can only come from you. You hold the key to everything within your own essence. I see that now.
You need space and a chance to breathe, process and open your heart.

I know that you are not afraid to confront your blocks, to own your actions and follow your heart. It is one of the reasons I love and admire you.

For me, I must not only trust you with my heart.
Trust that you are strong enough, intuitive enough, and spiritual enough to come through your journey stronger and better for it.
You will always be beautiful, warm and giving. If I really love you, I need to do just that,
love you. You will figure out the rest.

Rick

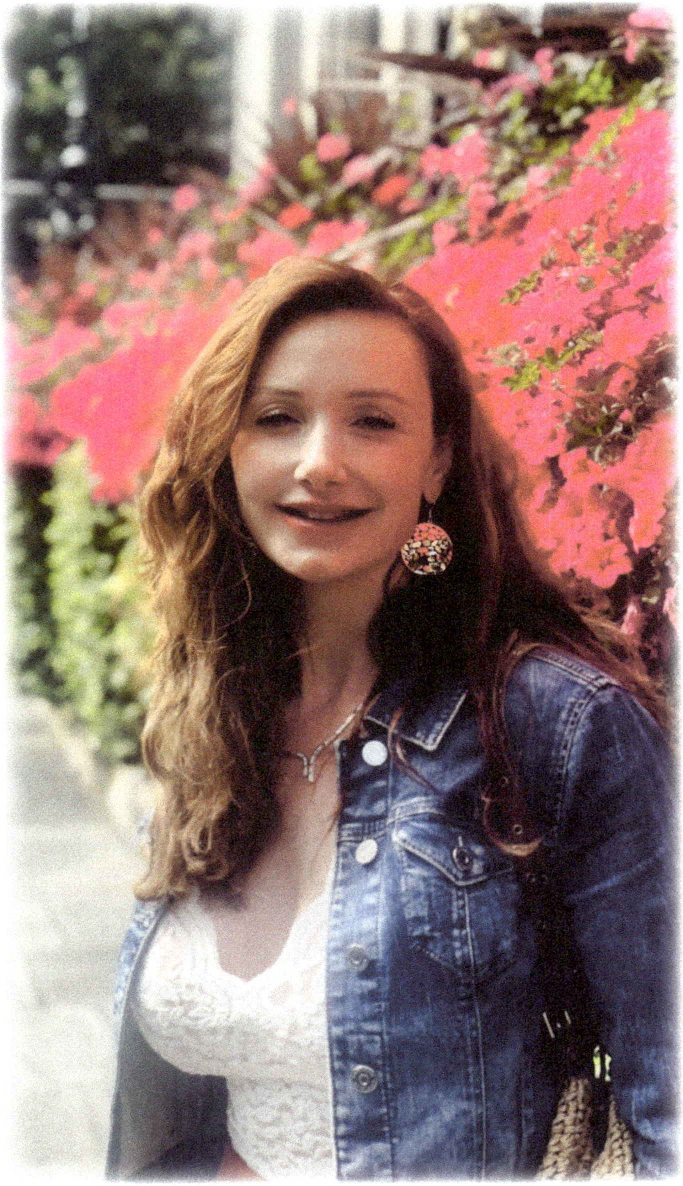

CHAPTER 32

Twin Flames

According to expert Todd Savvas, "A twin flame is your own soul shared across what appears to be two physical beings. It is one soul split into two physical beings. One soul split into two bodies". He goes on, "When a soul is created, it is split into two parts, mirrors of each other constantly yearning to reconnect".

Connecting with your twin flame is not a matter of luck. Finding your other half is a cosmic event, an alignment of the stars, the intervention of a higher being.

If blessed, it can speed up your personal growth, heal wounds, let go of blockers and lead you to self love.

Finding your other half can be incredibly challenging. It can bring out your most deep seeded insecurities, challenge your ego and require you to face your personal demons in order to greet your other half with unconditional true love.

When you meet your twin flame, there is a sense of recognition and intense attraction. The first time your paths cross, it feels like you have known each other for lifetimes. It is a puzzle where all the pieces come together and your life has new meaning.

Your emotions are amplified. Your feelings of love are stronger and sometimes overwhelming.

Because your twin flame is your mirror their purpose is to point out things that are sub-planting your personal growth.

Twin flames are inexplicably drawn to each other and their magnetic connection doesn't wane. It can be sexual but just as often a desire to be in that person's presence.

It's a relationship of growing pains, challenges and confrontation. It typically is not a Hollywood romantic movie. It forces both mirrors to confront and own parts of you that you don't like. Parts that you have probably buried until now.

Although there can be temporary setbacks and frustration, twin flames always find a way back to each other. Separation is never permanent. There is a sense of destiny in being together.

Savvas, a spiritual shaman, "The purpose of a twin flame relationship is to awaken you to your untapped potential and ignite a fire deep inside you. This relationship pushes you to do and be better and at the end of the day, it opens up a world of possibilities you never dreamt of."

Twin flames don't complete you. They are there to help you become the best version of yourself.

CHAPTER 33

Finding You

Jen,

I have been searching for you for years.
I realise now that in order to be blessed to be reunited with your other half you both must experience the necessary level of growth in order to be reunited
as one.

What are the odds that you and I could find your twin flame? With 8 billion people in the world, 197 countries and 7 continents, I found you.

It is the equivalent of picking the winning lottery numbers 37 weeks in a row. That is not luck. I know that it is divine intervention. It was meant to be. But for the life of me, I still don't know what I did to deserve you.

We were predestined, an event brought together by a higher power. I have a sense that we have known each other and have previously shared a life together in our past.

Our bond was immediate. It was more than instant recognition. I knew the moment I saw you that I was home.

I love you completely.

Rick

CHAPTER 34

The Same Direction

Jennifer,

I now know that love isn't just looking into each others eyes. It's the two of us looking in the same direction.

You are my future.
I am your forever.

Love has touched us and made our
connection sacred.

We are two bodies inhabited with a single
soul.

We can feel each other.
I am sensitive to your needs.
You read me. You understand me.
You are my heaven on earth.

You knew the hope of me. I know that you
believed that there was somebody out
there who would love you for you.
You believed that they would come into
your life and make everything right.

You never gave up on yourself or the promise of me. I found you. I'm here.
You don't need to hope anymore. It has happened and now we can get on with the rest of our lives.

Rick

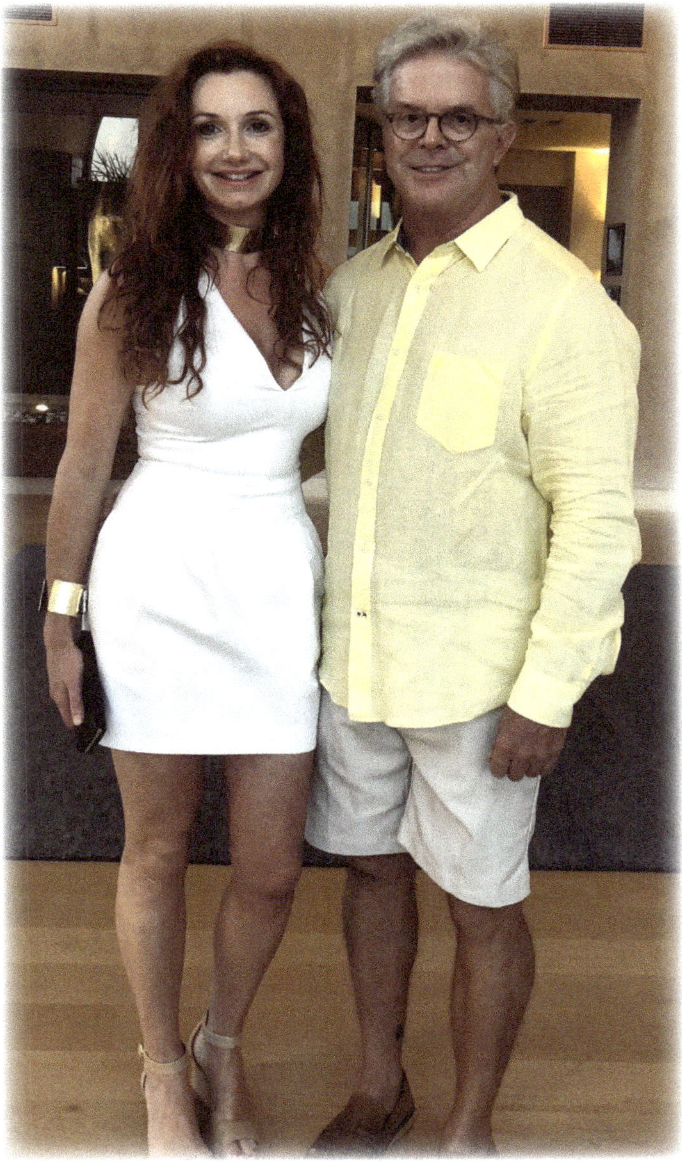

CHAPTER 35

Forever

Jennifer,

I dreamt last night that I asked you to marry me.

Your eyes said, "Yes".
Your heart said, "Forever".

Your soul said, " I found you again.
We are back together".

Rick

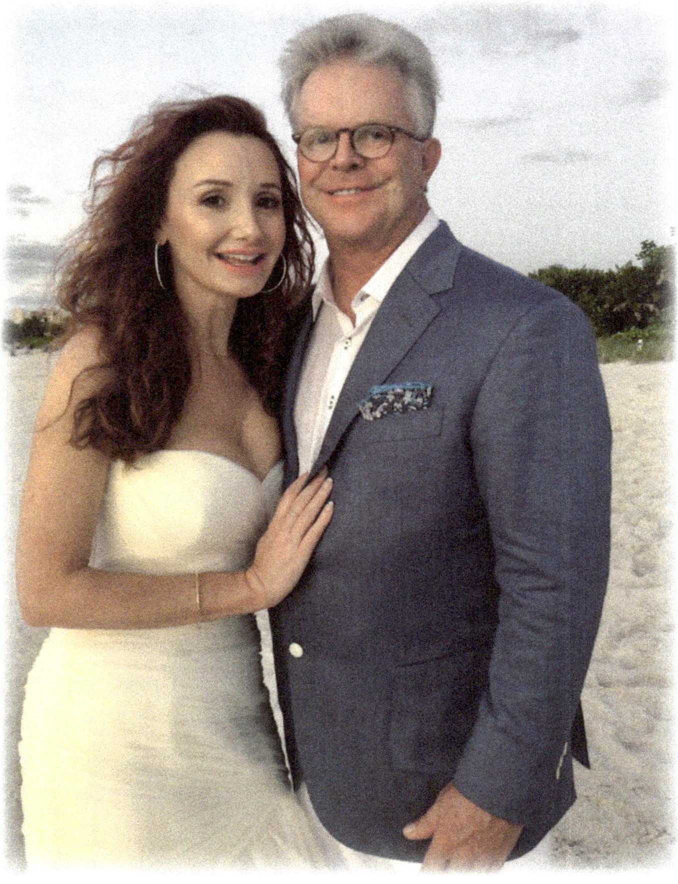

CHAPTER 36

Soulmate

"A person with whom you have an immediate connection the moment you meet."

A connection so strong that you are drawn to them in a way you have never experienced before. As this connection develops over time, you experience a love so deep, strong, and complex, that you begin to doubt that you ever truly loved anyone prior.

When I'm not around you, I am much more aware of the harshness of lifecycle But I am also aware of the beauty in life and you, Jen.

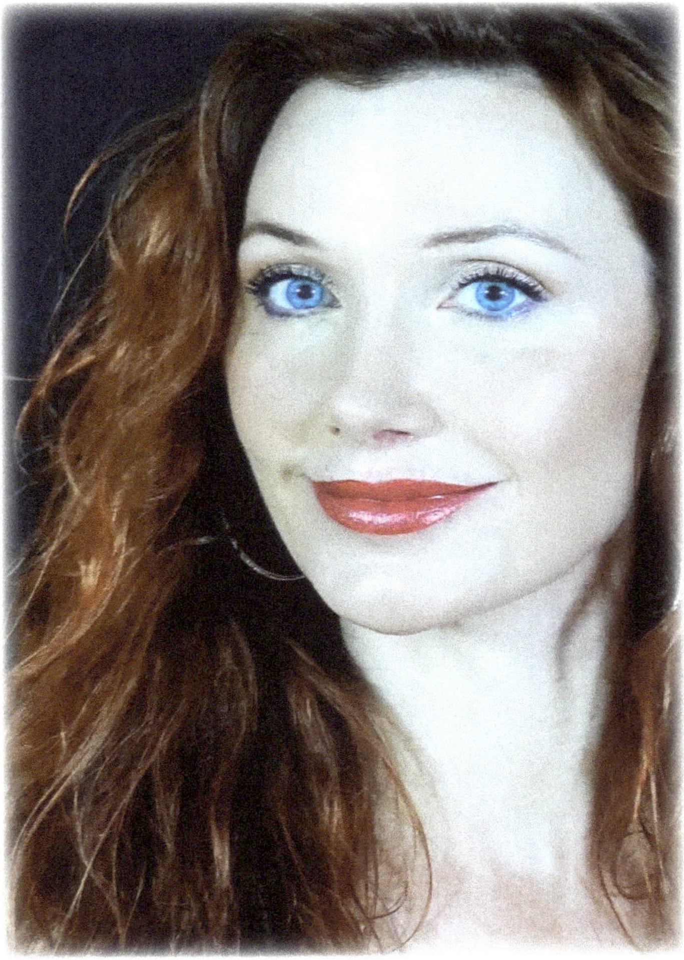

CHAPTER 37

Sharing One Soul

Jennifer,

I know that our souls met long before
our eyes did.
My existence is always in two places,
here and where you are.

You have changed the way my heart beats.
I see everything now through your eyes.
This is what happens when you begin to
share one soul with the love of your life.

If every time that I missed you,
a star fell from the sky,
It wouldn't take long and you would look
up at night and see blackness.

Fortunately, the power of my love for you
is what makes the sun rise every morning.

The most important gift in the world is
a relationship with that one person who
shares your values, your dreams,
your laughter, your love and your soul.

Few people find it.
 Even fewer understand
it's value until they lose it.
I am not one of them.
I will fight for your love.
I am the other half of your love story.

Rick

CHAPTER 38

Finding You Was Fate

Jen,

Because of you everything in my life has changed. I am more me than I have ever been. You have opened up parts of me that I didn't know existed.

I am the most romantic person I know because of you.
I have learned that in order to love unconditionally, you must love yourself unconditionally first.

You have made me curious again. You intellectually stimulate me. Our connection brings me alive. I love you not only for who you are but for what I am when I'm with you.

Finding you was fate. Being a part of your life was a choice. Falling completely in love with you was out of my control.

Do you hear me when I whisper, "I love you", under my breath?

Rick

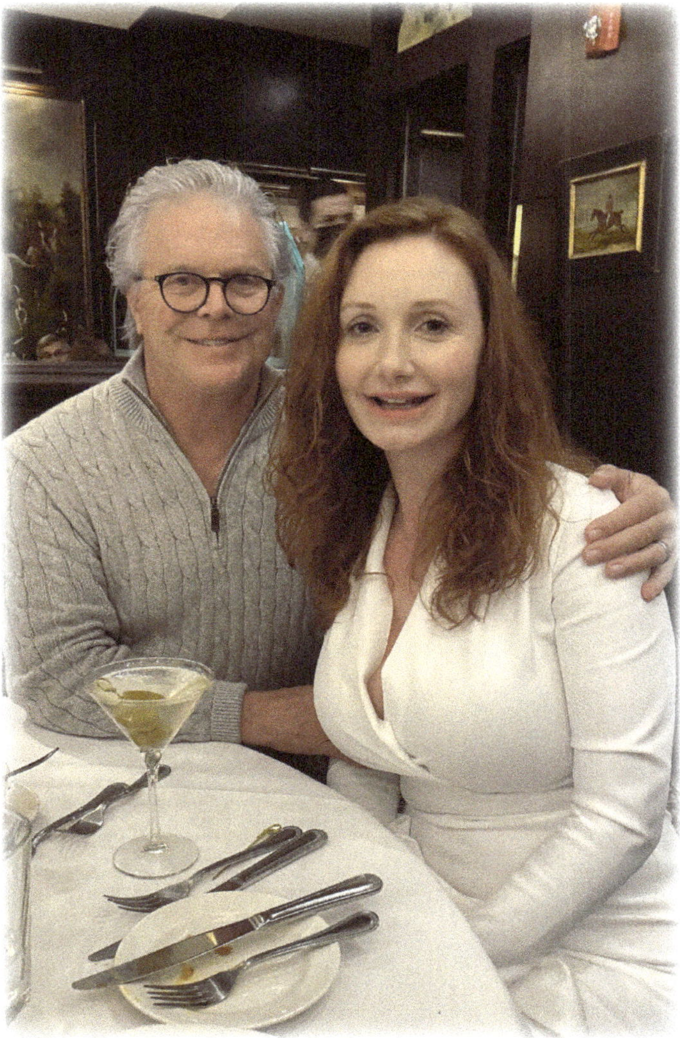

CHAPTER 39

You Own My Heart

Jen,

I know that love is an emotion that can only be felt because a million words cannot describe it.

My letters fall woefully short of painting a picture that could even remotely tell you just how much I care about and cherish you.

Because of you, I know now that there is a heaven.
And hell is not being with you each and every day.

We largely go through life numb.
Not truly feeling or connecting with each other.
We block out happiness to avoid the pain .

You have taught me that love is the cure
for the pain,
best given in massive doses
and administered with a kiss.

I am returning my heart to you, it's rightful
owner. I am home again.

Rick

CHAPTER 40

My Love Story

Jen,

You are my love story. I write you in to everything I do, everything I touch and all my dreams. You are the words that fill the chapters of our story.

I know that you and I are soulmates. It is exciting to find parts of yourself in someone else.

You have broken open my heart so new light can get in.

I have connected with you in ways that says, "I will love you for an eternity".

Rick

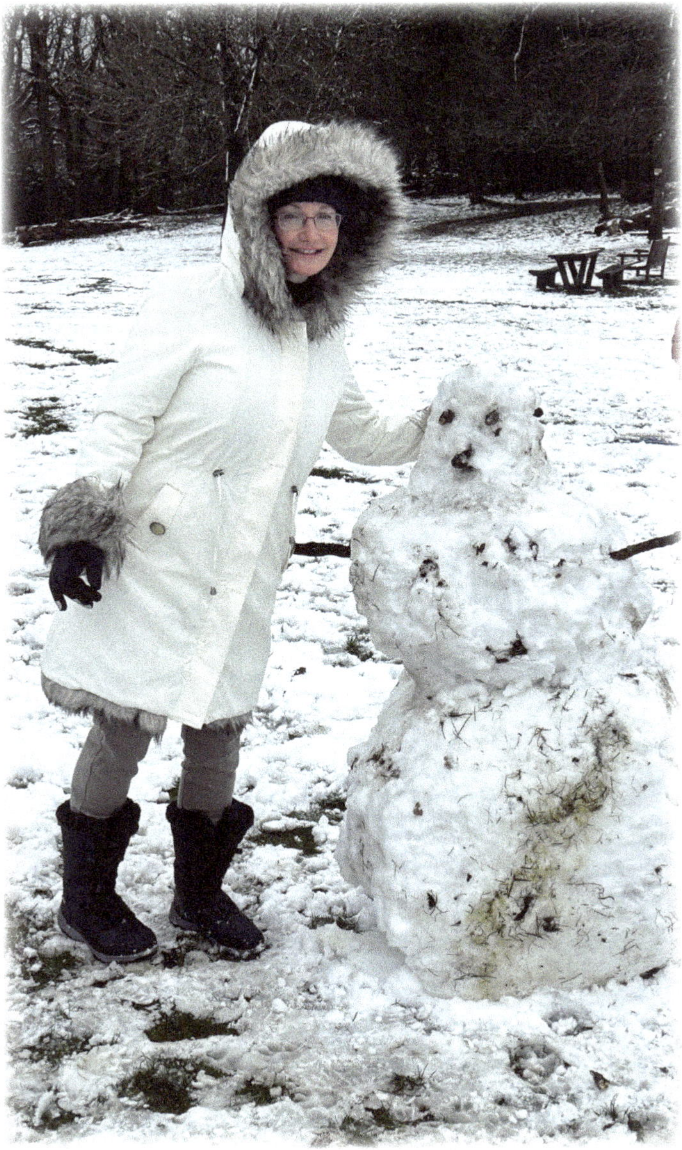

CHAPTER 41

Infinity

When we think of infinity we talk about
zero to forever.

But interestingly, you can take a number
like 1 and add .01, .02 and so on to create
infinity from a finite number.

Infinity within the finite.

And although we met in the autumn
of my life, I don't feel cheated.
What Jen has done is to give me a lifetime
of love and happiness in a finite period of time.

CHAPTER 42

Laughter

I love that Jen's laugh is funnier than my jokes.

There is no greater equalizer to anger and frustration than a smile and a good laugh.

A good laugh can be better than a hug. It is good when it comes from the heart and better when it comes from the belly.

It is said that, "Laughter is like a windshield wiper, it doesn't stop the rain but it allows you to keep going".

Remember Jen, "To laugh at yourself is to love yourself".

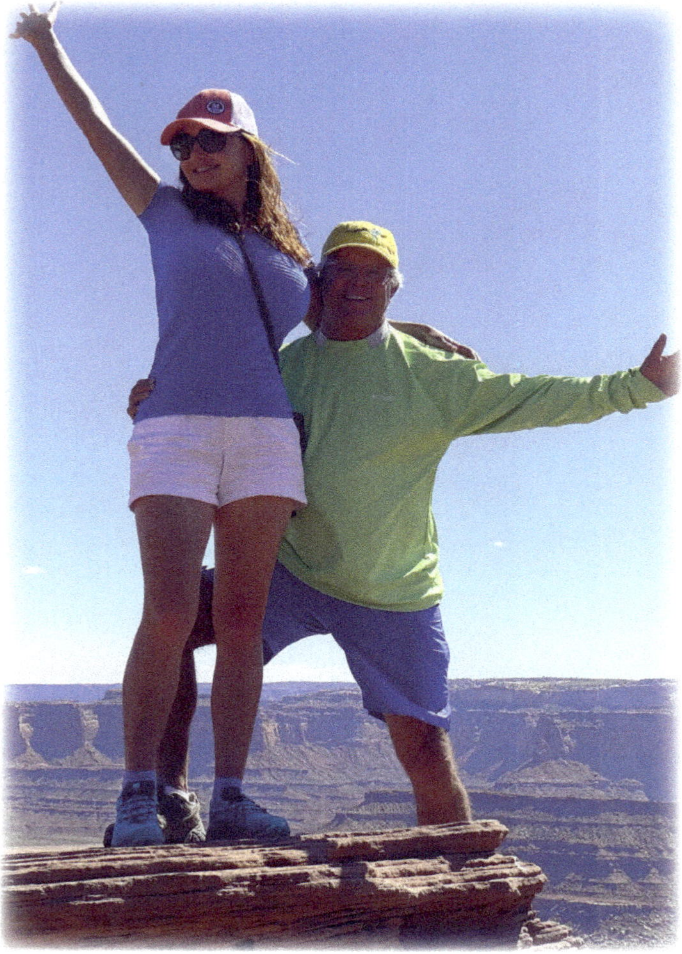

CHAPTER 43

Best Friends

Jen,
We talk like lovers,
We laugh like best friends

I just want you
All of you
Your beauty
Your flaws
Your giggles and laugh
Your heart and your soul

You are the angel that understands me.
Who really knows me and loves me anyway.

I want you to be my wife,
My lover
My best friend
The object of all my love and attention.

I look at you and see the rest of my life
in front of my eyes.
Rick

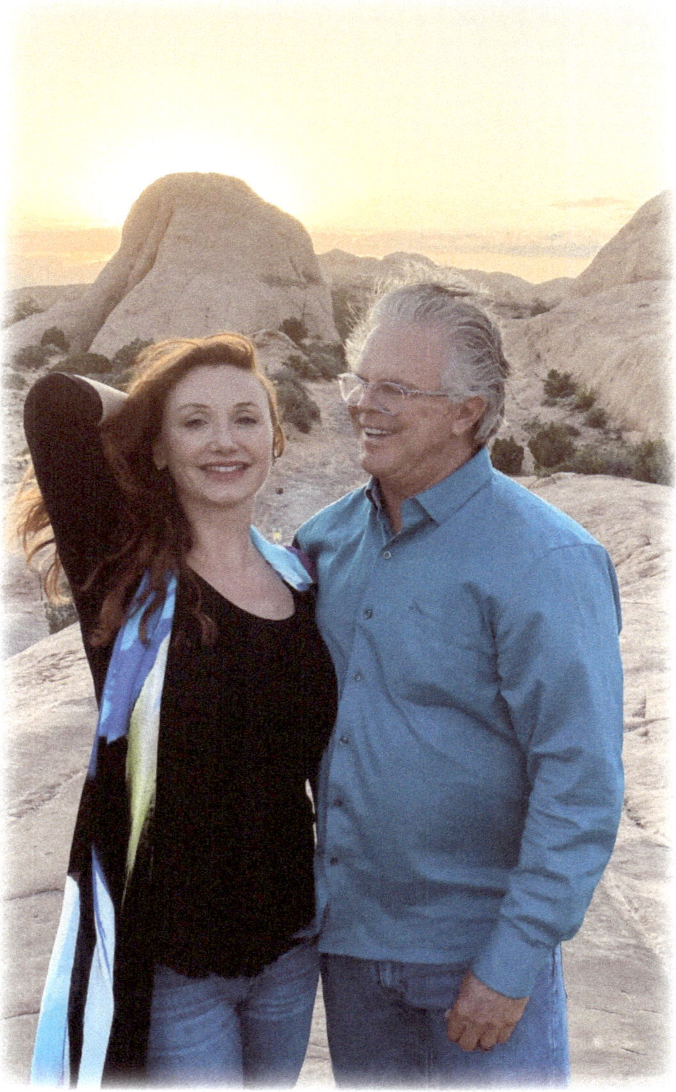

CHAPTER 44

Miracles

If you don't believe in miracles perhaps you have forgotten you are one.
Miracles happen around us everyday. We just need to take the time to look around to notice them.

God is in our lives. He touches us in so many ways. Through Him, we are born in love.

They don't always happen to you, but they many times may happen through you.

The great love that drew us together was a miracle.

As we live our life's, fear can find its way into our being. Our job is to overcome fear by recognizing that, as Gods greatest miracle,
we are born in love,
in His likeness and
can overcome anything.

Loving ourselves works miracles in our lives.

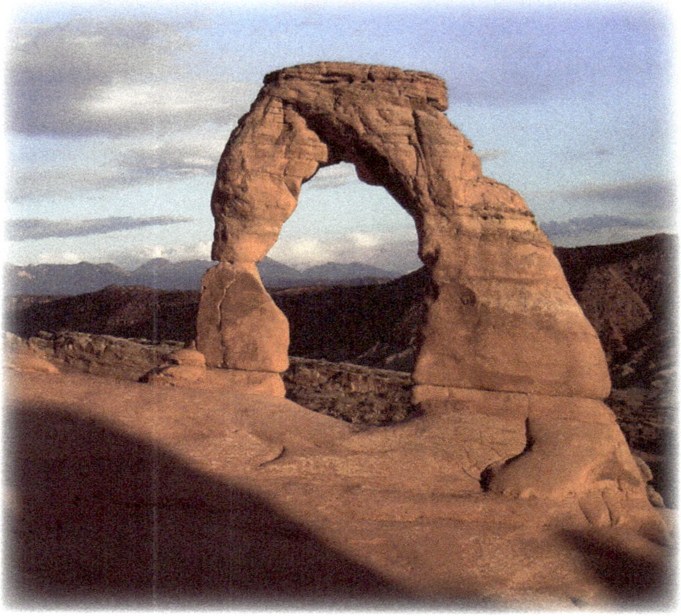

CHAPTER 45

Marry Me

Jen,

When I manifested you I was afraid
that it was only a dream.

When I met you I was afraid it
was only for a fleeting moment.

When I kissed you I was afraid
that it wouldn't last.

Now that I am marrying you I'm afraid
that it may only last one lifetime
instead of an eternity.

Rick

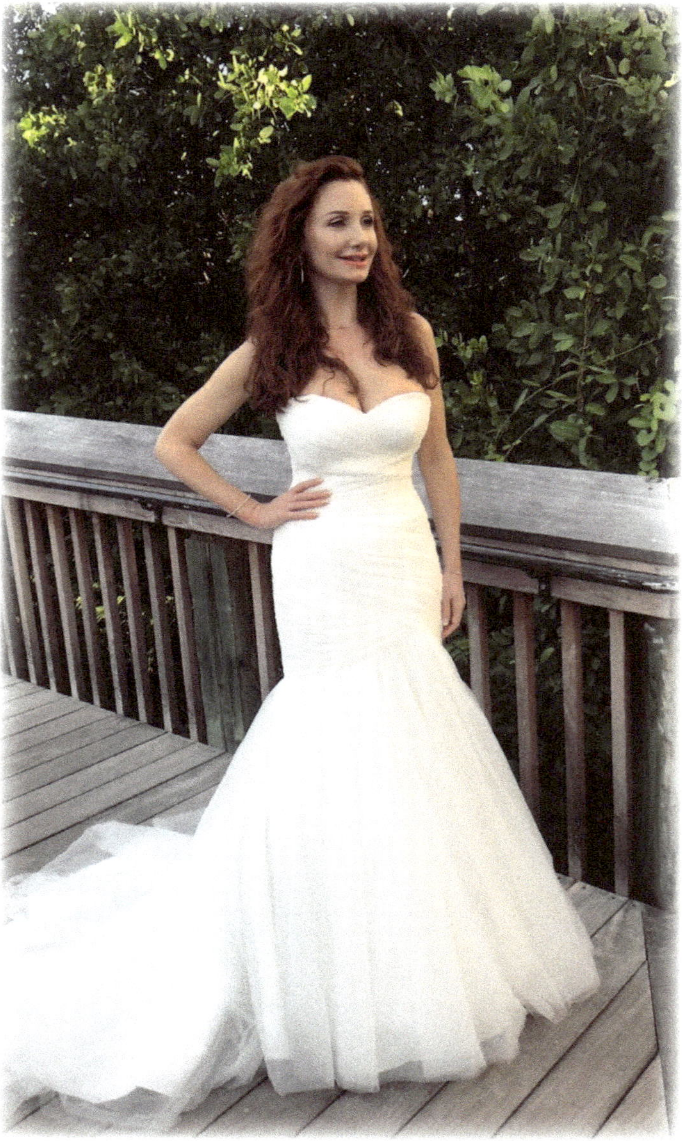

CHAPTER 46

"Us"

Jen,

My two favourite words are "Jennifer " and "us".

I am convinced that we do not find the meaning of life on our own. Like love, we find it together, within each other.

You are my epiphany. You have changed the trajectory of my life. I used to think that it showed strength to rely on yourself. I have now discovered that real strength is allowing yourself to be vulnerable. Real strength is loving you and losing myself in your heart.

Your goals have become my goals. Your growth has become my source of pride.

Your happiness is my happiness.
Yours and my dreams have combined to
become our dreams.

Rick

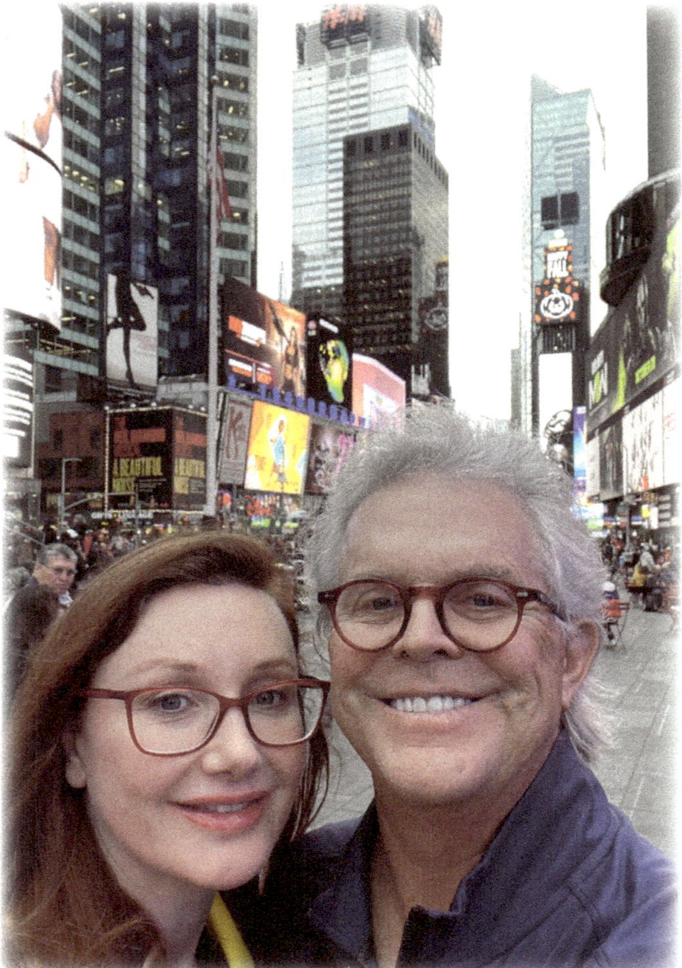

CHAPTER 47

Sleepovers

Jenny,

I laugh harder with you.

I look at you and see my best friend.
You are everything I've always wanted.
I trust you with my heart.
I feel more myself when I am with you.

Whether something good happens,
something funny happens or
even something crazy happens,
you are the one I look for to tell.

Marrying you would be like having a sleepover every night with your best friend.

I love you

Rick

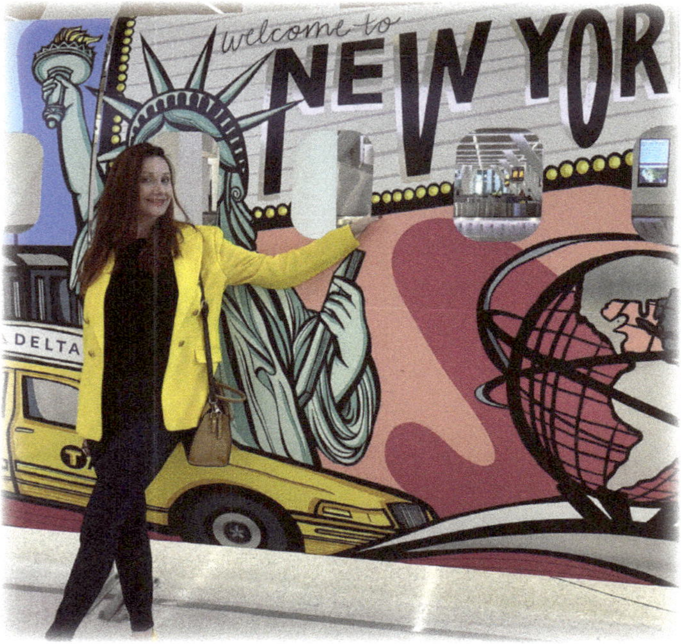
welcome to
NEW YOR
DELTA

CHAPTER 48

Sunsets

Jen,

I believe in magic.
I believe in you.
You are the reason
I believe in love.

If you ever wonder how far you can go,
just look how far you've come since
you put your hand in mine.

You are so beautiful, so special.
I'll always be there to remind you of that
in case you forget.

We will watch sunsets,
Let ocean waves caress our shoulders.
And see the world through your beautiful
blue eyes.

Rick

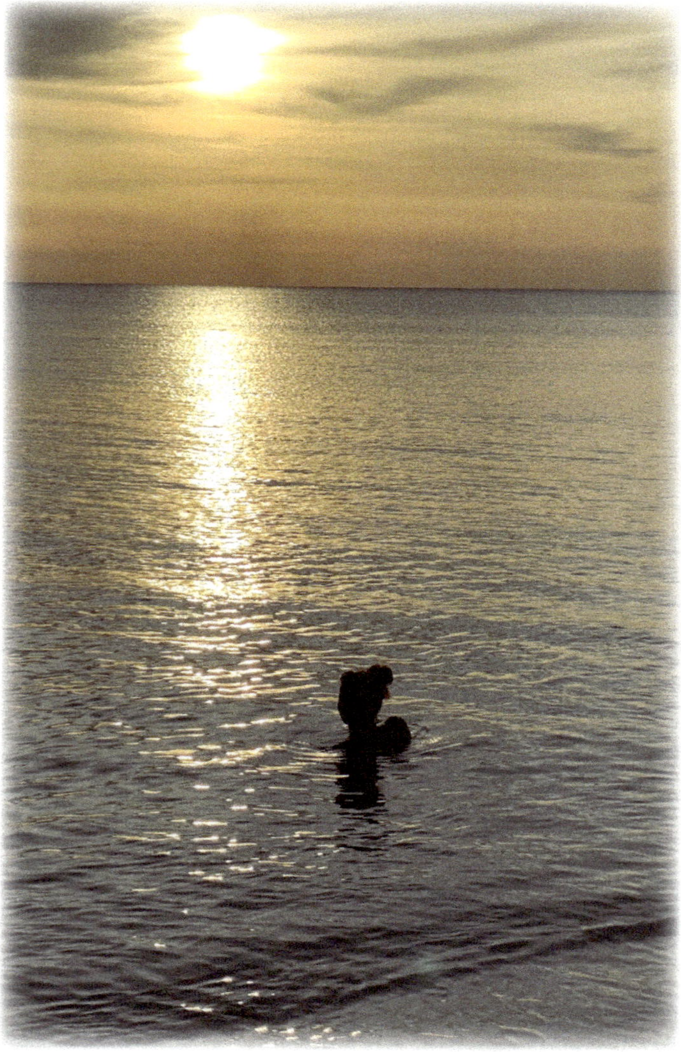

CHAPTER 49

Old Friends

Jen,

Whatever our souls are made of,
yours and mine are the same.
Our hearts are very old friends.

A long time ago you took a piece of me and I have spent years looking for you to make myself whole again in you.

I was not born whole. I was looking for my other half to become complete. In you, I can go home.

Our love becomes magic.

Rick

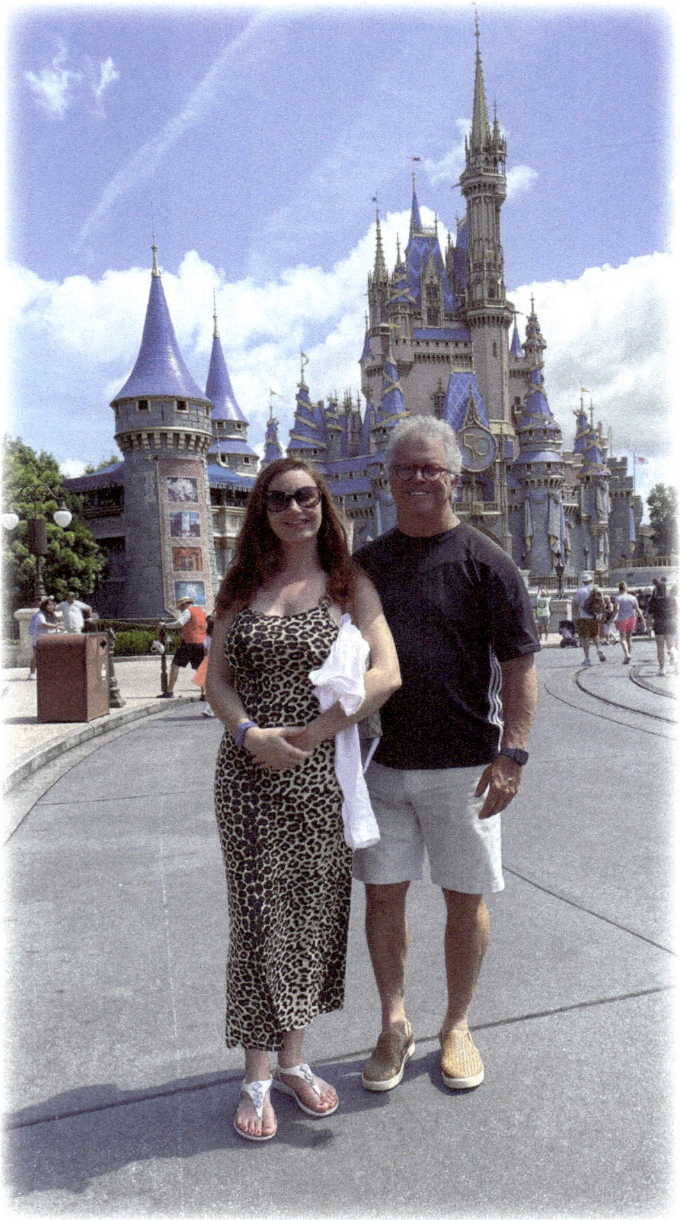

CHAPTER 50

Eternity

Jen,

Because of you, forever just doesn't seem long enough. Eternity is too finite.

With you, my love knows no boundaries, no distances, no fears.
I feel like I can conquer the world with one hand as long as I am holding yours with the other.
You make everything possible.

You are my beginning with no end.
You are the gift that I never deserved.

I love you, Jen, with everything that I am and with all that you helped me become.

Rick

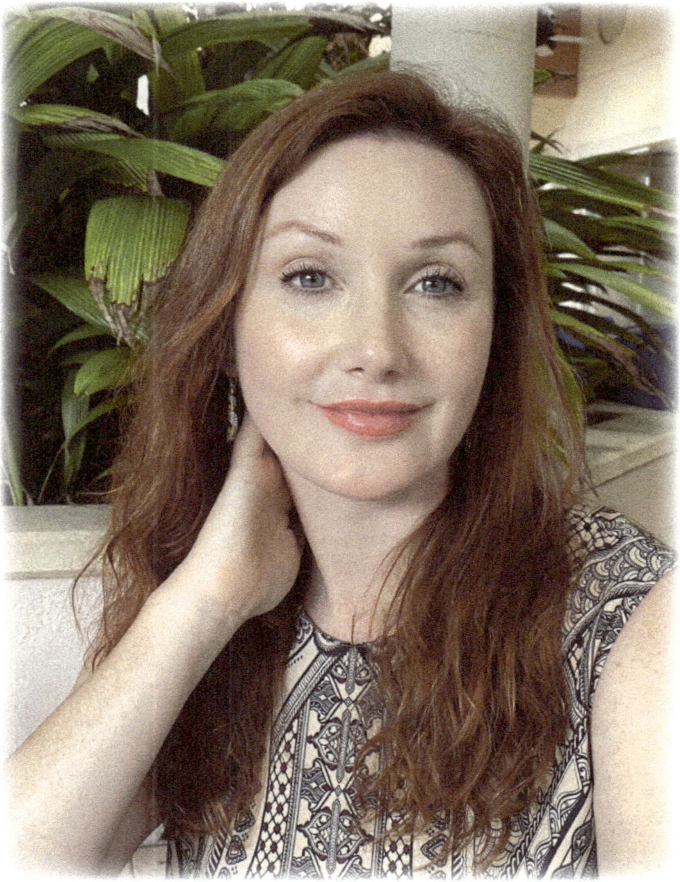

CHAPTER 51

Perfect

Jen,

Our journey may not be perfect but it is ours.
We are free to paint the portrait of what our lives were meant to be.

If we can dream it,
we can do it.
Because of you,
We can experience heaven on earth.

Whether we are exploring the world or sitting on the couch snuggling up with each other, our lives can be perfect because our love is perfect.

I love you and cherish every minute that you are in my life.

Rick

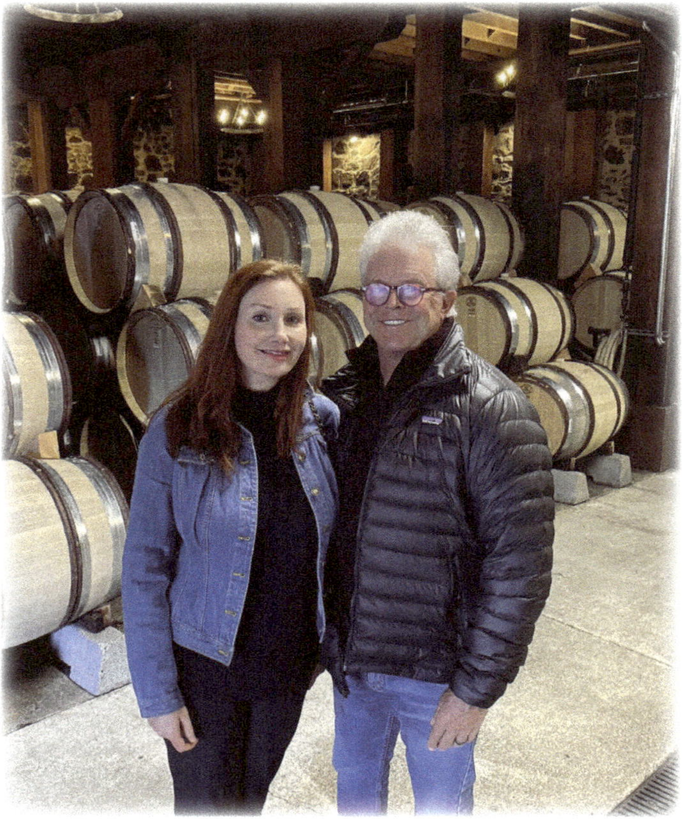

CHAPTER 52

Your Spirit

Jen,

Truly loving someone is seeing all the magic that they have within them and being there to remind them when they may forget just how special they are.

Not just to me but to the world. Your spirit has that kind of reach.

Loving you this way takes bravery.
Exposing your heart,
being this vulnerable
can be a scary thing.

It takes courage to love unconditionally but that is the kind of love that you deserve.
It is the kind of love you need. It says, "I love you just because. Be yourself, never change. You are perfect just the way you are. You are perfect for me".

Rick

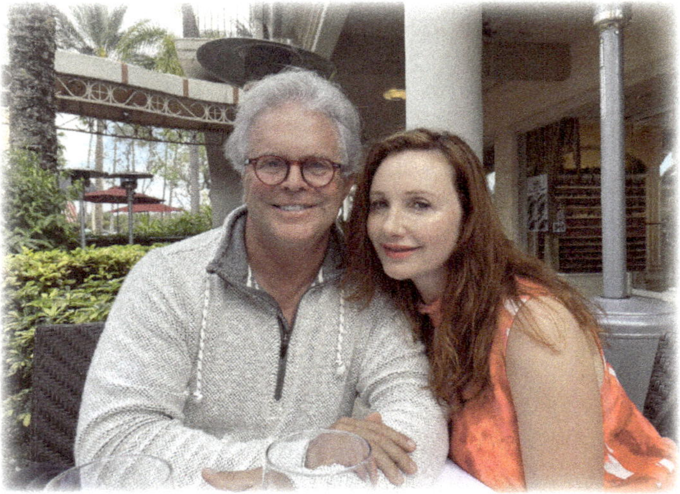

CHAPTER 53

The Miracle is You

Jenny,

Miracles happen when the heart opens.
My miracle was you.

Your heart opens and you know that everything you ever wanted had been inside you all along.

Close your eyes to old ends. Open your heart to new beginnings with me.

Your eyes tell me that you love me.
My hugs whisper for you to stay.

It's been a big step for us both. I am here to love and keep you safe. I want us. I want you to be my future.

We have the kind of love everyone dreams about. A life you deserve.

Rick

CHAPTER 54

Lifetimes

Jennifer,

Loving you has been the easiest thing I've ever done. Some people worry about keeping the flame going for years. I think about it in lifetimes.

You and I are different.
We are soulmates.
Each morning I wake up
loving you even more.
Every day I want you more.

We can't judge our relationship
on old experiences or through
the eyes of others.
They just don't have what is ours.

I adore you

Rick

112

CHAPTER 55

My Reset

Jennifer,

You are my reset. I get to live my life again with you. And every day with you becomes the greatest day of my life.

You are my very reason for breathing.
You are every dream that I've ever had.

Simply put, I am permanently in love with you.
I loved you from the first moment that I saw you. And before that, I was in love with the promise of you

In you, I have found my place in eternity.

It is wonderful to have fallen in love with an angel.

Rick

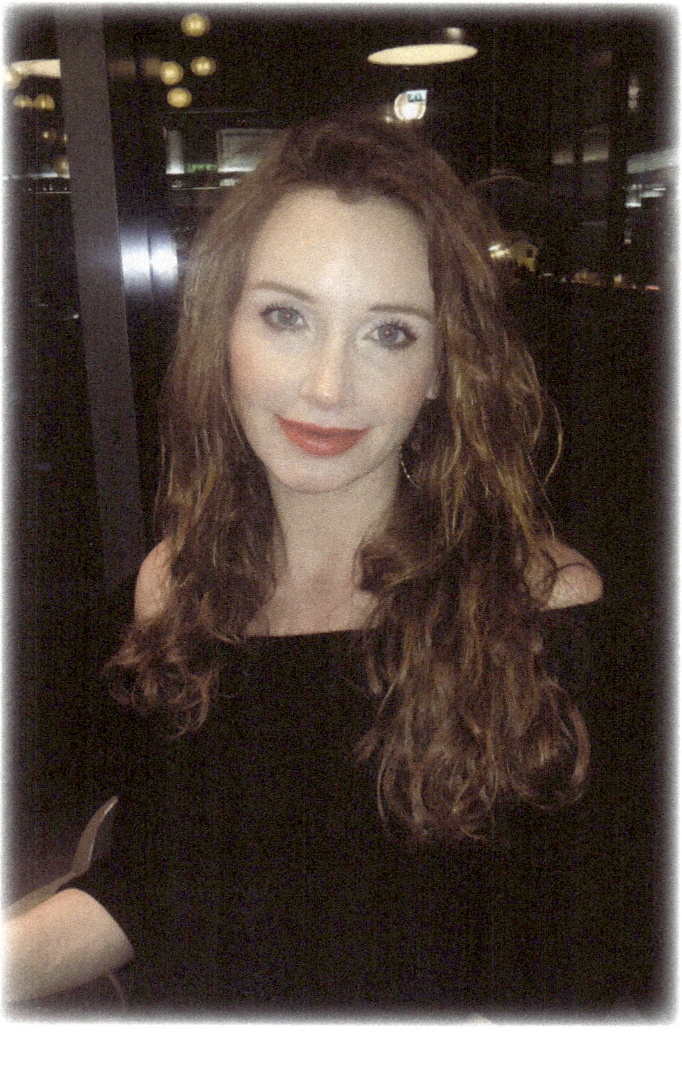

CHAPTER 56

Only Goodnight

My Jen,

The soul knows nothing of distance. To the soul, time is meaningless. It understands only resonance, energy and feeling.

It doesn't matter how far away you are or for how long. That energy will guide us back to each other.

My arms will hold you in the present.
My words will unlock a future that is ours.

As wonderful as our time together has been, I know that our best days are still ahead.

Soon we will never have to say goodbye again, only goodnight.

Love
Rick

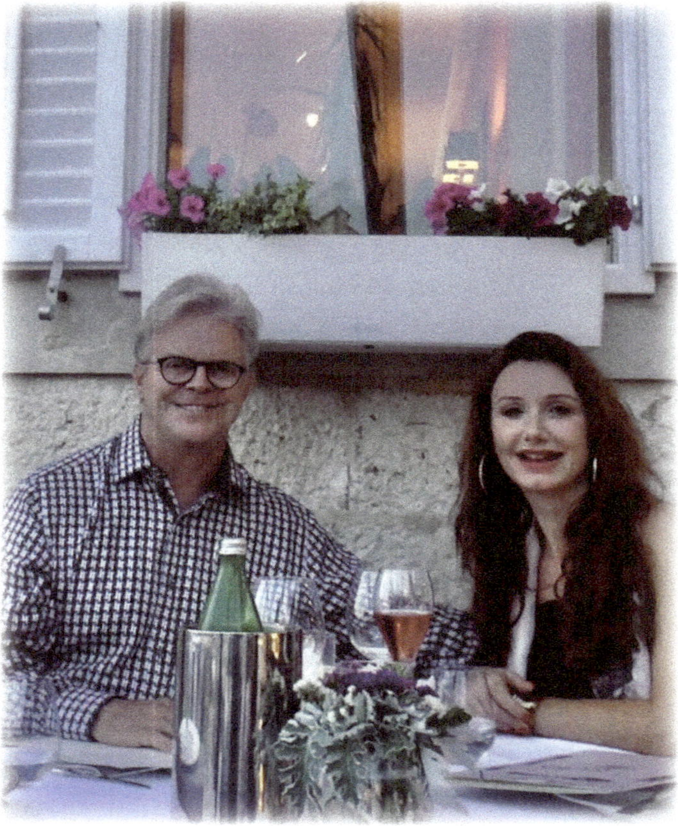

CHAPTER 57

Connection

Jen,
I don't love you with just my heart.
My heart can stop beating.
I can't love you with just my mind for it can forget.

I love you with my soul.
It is eternal.
It transcend lifetimes.
It never dies.
It never forgets.

I am your twin flame. That means loving you forever. It means that you are my best friend and a part of me. I'll will always love and cherish you. We connect at every level,
in every way.

Not only do you make me better.
You make me want to be better.
With you I don't need to compromise.

Rick

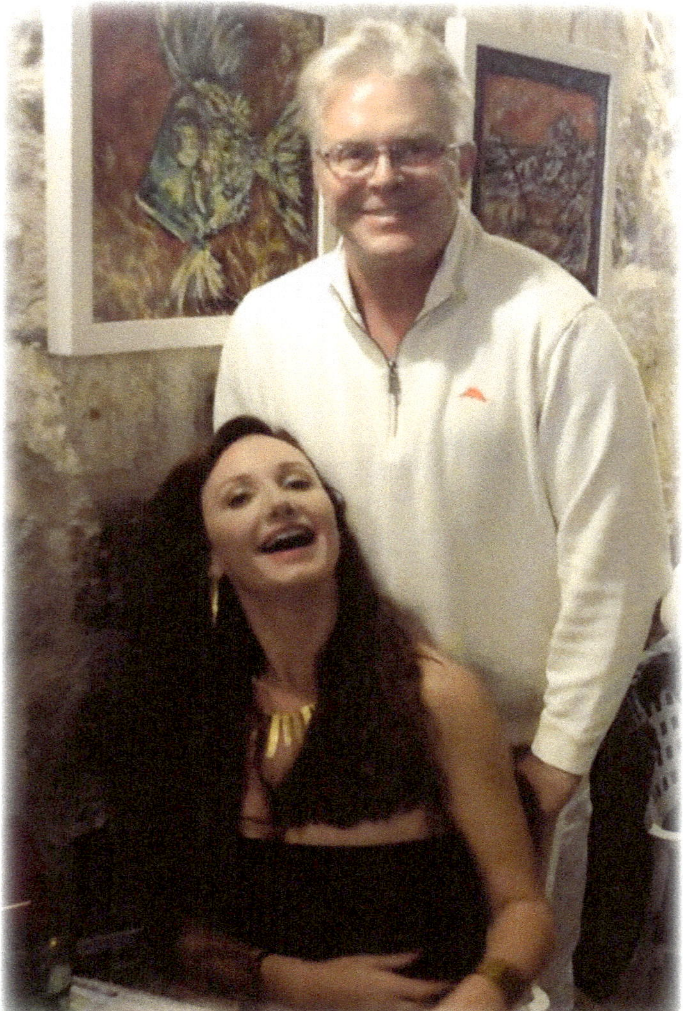

CHAPTER 58

Shout!

Jenny,

You are my best friend. You are every breath I take. You are the smile on my face. You make me want to shout your name for everyone to hear.

There is an energy that people can't help but react to when we are together. As one, we can experience a love that most people only dream about.

A love that lasts forever.

Rick

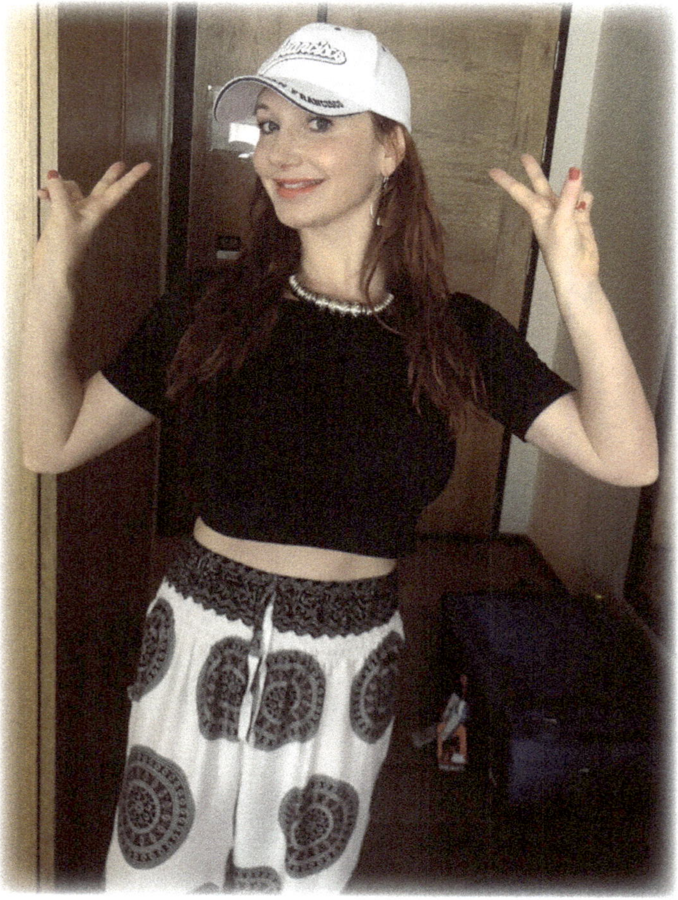

CHAPTER 59

Life Together

Jenny,

You are my love story. I write you into everything I do. My love for you, your love for me is what fills these pages.

When we have transcended to another life together, these words will be there so others may comprehend just how much you mean to me.

I will love you to the moon,

Rick

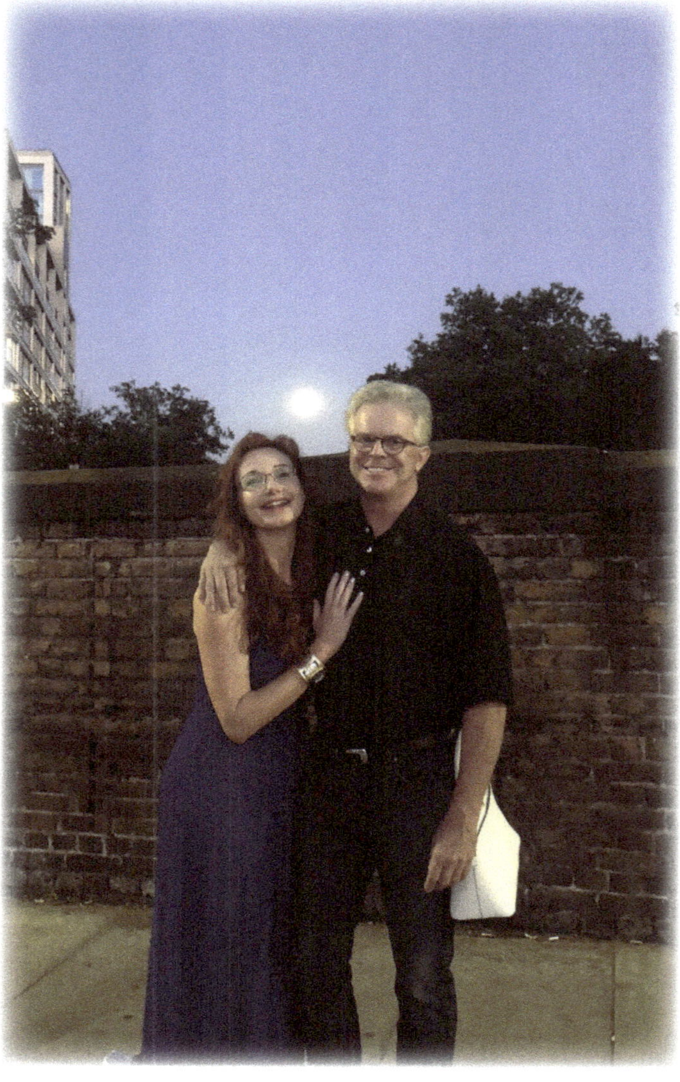

CHAPTER 60

True Love Stories

Jennifer,

This is a book that will go on forever.
True love stories have no endings.

You are affixed in my heart.
I have carried you with me for years.
You are a part of me.
And in finding you I actually have found myself.
Until I found you I didn't even know I was lost.

People say that you really only fall in love once.
It's not true. I fall in love with you all over again,
every time I see you, each time we talk.

I'm not writing a love story. You and I are making one.
True love isn't about ego. It's not about insecurity.
It's loving someone and putting their needs above all else.
I would do anything to make you happy
and your love is my reward.

Rick

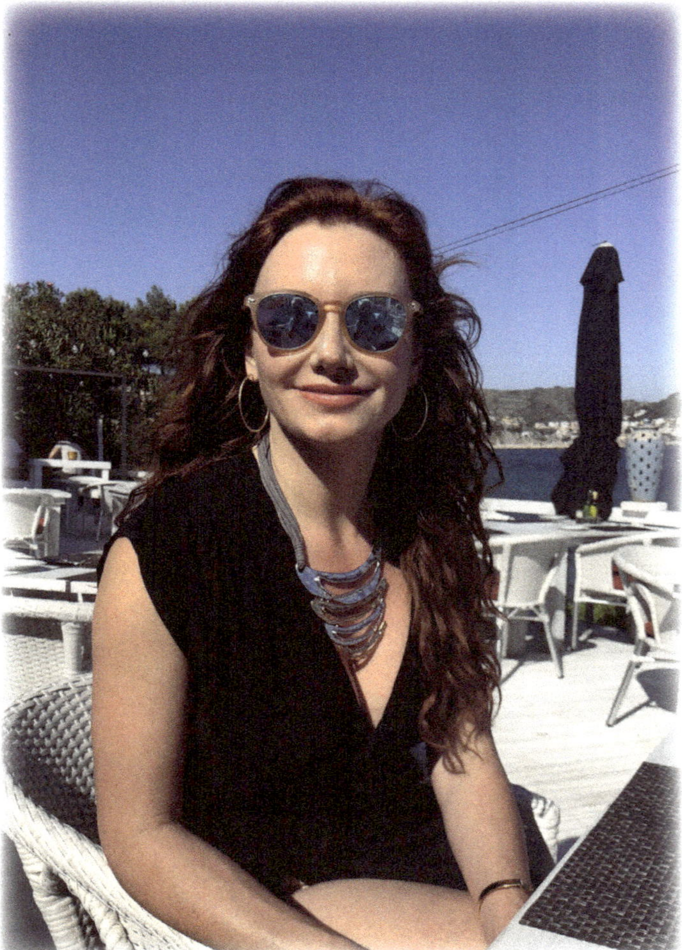

CHAPTER 61

What's Next

Jen,

You asked me what I would want come back as in my next life. I said, "Your cat". But that's not really true.

My only regret is that we met too late and I didn't have the opportunity to spend my entire life next to you. So when I come back, I want to be that 5 year old boy who moves next door to you. You are a few months older than me. I'm a Gemini and you are an Aquarius.

I'll be your best friend. We will walk to the bus stop every morning. Sometimes I'll hold your hand. We will share an umbrella on rainy days. You usually sit with your girlfriends but I'll always be close by to make sure you are okay.

Your parents are glad we are so close. They sense that I somehow will protect you and keep you safe.

You're smarter than me and I let you help me with my school work. The truth is I just want to be close to you.

There will be fights and disagreements because that is life. But deep down inside I know that I can't be angry with you. Even at a young age I know that you have my heart.

Then there was our first kiss. The other kids dared us to do it. I pretended that I didn't like it but you knew I did. When the neighborhood kids play games I always pick you first for my team. I guess I feel like a winner when you are next to me.

Every year we look to see if we are in the same classes. You are so pretty and have lots of friends. I have the same friends too, because of you. Sometimes we pretend like we are married. Our little brother and sisters are our kids. You are the boss of the house. Everyone listens to you.

It's because of you that Valentines Day is my favorite holiday.

We continue on our journey. There are other boys who are trying to win your affection.
Although it makes me jealous, I know that somehow things will work out.

I write you love notes. You giggle and show them to your friends. It embarrasses me but I keep passing them on to you. I can't help myself. If I don't tell you how I feel, I'll bust!

High school dances, Friday night dates; everyone knows I'm your guy. We kiss, we hold each other, we dance and we love. There are ups and downs and there are times that we break up. You feel free for awhile but as twin flames we always seem to find our way back to each other.

You are bubbly, light and have a real zest for life. I admire and am energized by you. We are always at each others houses. Evenings sitting on the front porch talking about nothing; talking about everything. Our families are tied together by our love for each other. I knew that it was always you. It felt like I had been married to you for lifetimes.

College felt like our honeymoon. Away from watchful eyes, we were free to be together to explore and experience each other in the most intimate ways. I am studying harder than ever.
I understand that I'm working for our future. Between classes, parties and nights out, there are quiet evenings together.

We know that we are going to get married. We talk about it all the time. You want three kids.
I want ten. For some crazy reason you want to name our son Raylan James and our daughters Elizabeth Marie and Barbara Nicole. I don't know how you came up with them but I've learned that there is no sense in arguing with you! We have our whole lives in front of us and somehow it all feels predestined.

When you put your head on the pillow tonight, know that I am next to you, kissing your lips and stroking your hair. I am in your heart and whispering in your ear, "I love you".

Rest easy knowing that I am with you always and know that we will be together in your dreams. Sooner than you think we will be back together in our next life.

I'll be waiting for you at the bus stop. You'll recognize me. I'm the one holding your hand.